Anonymous

The New Jubilee Harp

Or, christian hymns and songs: a new collection of hymns and tunes for public and social worship

Anonymous

The New Jubilee Harp
Or, christian hymns and songs: a new collection of hymns and tunes for public and social worship

ISBN/EAN: 9783337290733

Printed in Europe, USA, Canada, Australia, Japan

Cover: Foto ©Lupo / pixelio.de

More available books at **www.hansebooks.com**

WINNOWED HYMNS:

A COLLECTION OF

SACRED SONGS,

ESPECIALLY ADAPTED FOR REVIVALS, PRAYER

AND CAMP MEETINGS.

Rev. C. C. McCABE and Rev. D. T. MACFARLAN,
EDITORS.

NEW YORK AND CHICAGO:
PUBLISHED BY
BIGLOW & MAIN, (Successors to WM. B. BRADBURY.)
NELSON & PHILLIPS, 805 Broadway, New York.
NATIONAL PUBLISHING ASSOCIATION FOR THE PROMOTION OF HOLINESS, 14 North Seventh St., Philadelphia.
FOR SALE BY BOOKSELLERS AND MUSIC DEALERS.

Entered, according to Act of Congress, in the Year 1873, by BIGLOW & MAIN, in the office of the Librarian of Congress, at Washington.

PREFACE.

IT is not presumed that *all* the wheat from the great harvest of song has been gathered into this little garner.

We simply claim that no chaff is here.

In compiling "**Winnowed Hymns**" we have yielded to a long cherished desire to collect our favorites from many books into one.

Our object has been to select such hymns as will be found intensely devotional, therefore we do not hesitate to say that "**Winnowed Hymns**" will prove one of the most valuable works ever issued for Camp Meetings, Praise and Social Meetings.

We confess to a great desire that our little book should be extensively used at the *Family Altar*. Holy song should always constitute part of our worship there. No pressure of business, no household cares should ever cause the omission of a song of praise to Him "who maketh for us the out-going of the morning and evening to rejoice."

We have endeavored to make "**Winnowed Hymns**" in every respect what its title would convey—a compilation of the best selections from the extensive copyrights of the Publishers and others, embracing the never-to-be-forgotten songs of WM. B. BRADBURY, I. B. WOODBURY, Rev. R. LOWRY, W. H. DOANE, S. J. VAIL, HUBERT P. MAIN, WM. G. FISCHER, ASA HULL, Rev. L. HARTSOUGH, &c., &c.

We desire to make special acknowledgement of kind services and valuable suggestions rendered to us by Rev. W. MCDONALD, Mr. JOHN C. MIDDLETON and others, and for the deep interest taken by them in the success of this work.

C. C. McCABE,
D. T. MACFARLAN.

I need Thee every hour.

Mrs. A. S. HAWKS.
Rev. ROBERT LOWRY.
From "Royal Diadem," by per.

1. I need thee every hour, Most gra-cious Lord; No tender voice like
2. I need thee every hour; Stay thou near by; Temptations lose their
3. I need thee every hour, In joy or pain; Come quickly and a-
4. I need thee every hour; Teach me thy will; And thy rich promis-
5. I need thee every hour, Most Ho-ly One; Oh, make me thine in-

thine Can peace af - ford.
pow'r When thou art nigh.
bide, Or life is vain.
es In me ful - fill.
deed, Thou bless-ed Son.

REFRAIN.

I need thee, oh! I need thee; Every hour I need thee; O bless me now, my Sav-iour! I come to thee.

4 Safe in the Arms of Jesus.

FANNY J. CROSBY, 1868.
W. H. DOANE.
From "Songs of Devotion," by per.

1. Safe in the arms of Je - sus, Safe on his gentle breast,
2. Safe in the arms of Je - sus, Safe from corroding care,
3. Je - sus, my heart's dear re-fuge, Je - sus has died for me;

Cho.—*Safe in the arms of Je - sus, Safe on his gen - tle breast,*

There by his love o'er-shad - ed, Sweetly my soul shall rest.
Safe from the world's temptations, Sin cannot harm me there.
Firm on the Rock of A - ges Ev - er my trust shall be.
There by his love o'er-shad - ed, Sweet-ly my soul shall rest.

Hark, 'tis the voice of an - gels, Borne in a song to me,
Free from the blight of sor - row, Free from my doubts and fears;
Here let me wait with patience, Wait till the night is o'er;

O - ver the fields of glo - ry, O - ver the jas - per sea.
On - ly a few more tri - als, On - ly a few more tears!
Wait till I see the morning Break on the golden shore.

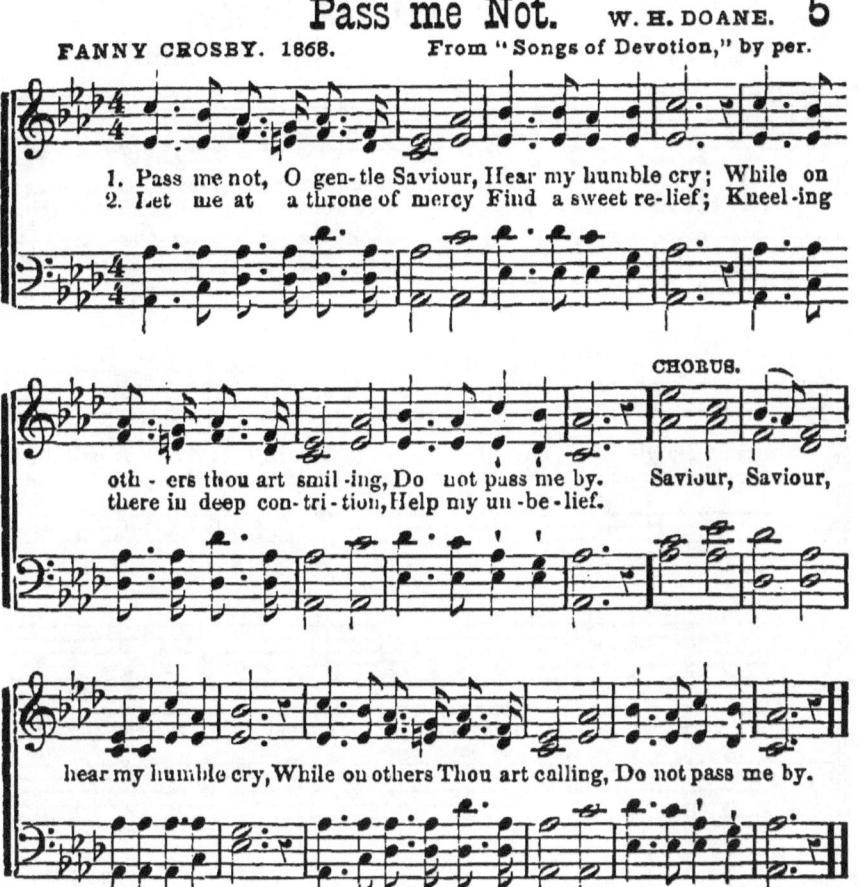

3.

Trusting only in thy merit,
　Would I seek thy face;
Heal my wounded, broken spirit,
　Save me by thy grace.
　　Cho.—Saviour, Saviour, &c.

4.

Thou, the spring of all my comfort,
　More than life to me;
Whom have I on earth beside thee?
Whom in heaven but thee?
　　Cho.—Saviour, Saviour, &c.

6 I Love to tell the Story.

KATE HANKEY. Wm. G. FISCHER, by per.

1. I love to tell the story Of un-seen things a-bove, Of Je-sus and his glo-ry, Of Je-sus and his love, I love to tell the story Because I know 'tis true; It sat-is-fies my longings As nothing else can do.
2. I love to tell the story; More wonderful it seems Than all the gold-en fan-cies Of all our gold-en dreams. I love to tell the story It did so much for me! And that is just the rea-son I tell it now to thee.

CHORUS.

I love to tell the sto-ry, 'Twill be my theme in glo-ry, To tell the old, old sto-ry, Of Je-sus and his love.

More Love to Thee, O Christ. 7

Words by Mrs. E. PRENTISS.
W. H. DOANE.
From "Songs of Devotion," by per.

1. More love to Thee, O Christ! More love to Thee; Hear Thou the pray'r I make
2. Once earthly joy I craved. Sought peace and rest; Now Thee alone I seek,
3. Let sorrow do its work, Send grief and pain; Sweet are Thy messengers,

On bended knee; This is my earnest plea, More love, O Christ, to Thee,
Give what is best: This all my pray'r shall be, More love, O Christ, &c.
Sweet their refrain. When they can sing with me, More love, O Christ, &c.

More love to Thee! More love to Thee!

4 Then shall my latest breath
Whisper Thy praise;
This be the parting cry
My heart shall raise;
This still its prayer shall be
More love, O Christ, to Thee!
More love to Thee!
More love to Thee!

Tune, "I LOVE TO TELL THE STORY," page 6.

3 I love to tell the story;
'Tis pleasant to repeat
What seems, each time I tell it,
More wonderfully sweet.
I love to tell the story;
For some have never heard
The message of salvation
From God's own holy word. *Cho.*

4 I love to tell the story;
For those who know it best
Seem hungering and thirsting
To hear it like the rest.
And when, in scenes of glory,
I sing the new, new song,
'Twill be—the old, old story
That I have loved so long. *Cho.*

8. The Precious Name.

Mrs. LYDIA BAXTER.
W. H. DOANE.
From "Pure Gold," by per

1. Take the name of Je-sus with you, Child of sorrow and of woe—
2. Take the name of Je-sus ev-er, As a shield from every snare;

It will joy and comfort give you, Take it then where'er you go.
If temptations 'round you gather, Breathe that holy name in pray'r.

CHORUS.

Precious name, O how sweet! Hope of earth and joy of heaven, Precious name, O how sweet—Hope of earth and Joy of heav'n.

Precious name, O how sweet, how sweet,

3 Oh! the precious name of Jesus;
 How it thrills our souls with joy,
When His loving arms receive us,
And His songs our tongues employ. *Cho.*

4 At the name of Jesus bowing,
 Falling prostrate at His feet,
King of kings in heav'n we'll crown Him,
When our journey is complete. *Cho.*

Safe within the Vail. 9

Rev. E. ADAMS. Arr. from J. M. EVANS.

1. "Land a-head!" its fruits are waving O'er the hills of fadeless green; And the liv-ing waters laving Shores where heav'nly forms are seen.
2. Onward, bark! the cape I'm rounding; See the bless-ed wave their hands; Hear the harps of God resounding From the bright immortal bands.

CHORUS.
Rocks and storms I'll fear no more, When on that e-ter-nal shore; Drop the an-chor! Furl the sail! I am safe within the vail!

3.
There, "let go the anchor," riding
On this calm and silv'ry bay;
Sea-ward fast the tide is gliding,
Shores in sunlight stretch away.
Cho.

4.
Now we're safe from all temptation,
All the storms of life are past;
Praise the Rock of our salvation,
We are safe at home at last!—*Cho.*

10 At the Cross there's Room.

FANNY J. CROSBY, 1871.
Rev. R. LOWRY.
From "Royal Diadem." by per.

1. Mourner, whereso-e'er thou art, *At the cross there's room:* Tell the burden of thy heart; *At the cross there's room;* Tell it in thy Saviour's ear, Cast away thine every fear, Only speak, and He will hear; *At the cross there's room.*

2 Haste thee, wanderer, tarry not;
  At the cross there's room;
Seek that consecrated spot;
  At the cross there's room;
Heavy laden, sore oppressed,
Love can soothe thy troubled breast;
In the Saviour find thy rest;
  At the cross there's room!

3 Thoughtless sinner, come to-day;
  At the cross there's room;
Hark! the Bride and Spirit say,
  At the cross there's room;
Now a living fountain see,
Opened there for you and me,
Rich and poor, for bond and free;
  At the cross there's room!

4 Blessed thought! for every one
  At the cross there's room;
Love's atoning work is done;
  At the cross there's room;
Streams of boundless mercy flow,
Free to all who thither go;
O that all the world might know,
  At the cross there's room!

The Gate Ajar for Me. 11

Mrs. LYDIA BAXTER.
S. J. VAIL. "From Singing Annual,"
By per. of PHILIP PHILLIPS.

1. There is a gate that stands a-jar, And, thro' its por-tals gleaming,
A radiance from the Cross a-far The Saviour's love re-veal-ing.

REFRAIN.
Oh, depths of mer-cy! can it be That gate was left a-jar for me?
For me..... for me?.... Was left a-jar for me?
For me, for me?

2 That gate ajar stands free for all
   Who seek through it salvation;
The rich and poor, the great and small,
   Of every tribe and nation. *Refr.*

3 Press onward, then, though foes may frown,
   While mercy's gate is open,
Accept the cross, and win the crown,
   Love's everlasting token. *Refr.*

4 Beyond the river's brink we'll lay
   The Cross that here is given,
And bear the Crown of life away,
   And love Him more in heaven. *Refr.*

12   The Valley of Blessing.

Words by ANNIE WITTENMYER.   Music by WM. G. FISCHER.

1 I have entered the valley of blessing so sweet,
   And Jesus abides with me there;
   And his spirit and blood make my cleansing complete,
   And his perfect love casteth out fear.

CHORUS.

O, come to this valley of blessing so sweet,
   Where Jesus will fullness bestow—
Oh   believe, and receive, and confess him,
   That all his salvation may know.

2 There is peace in the valley of blessing so sweet,
   And plenty the land doth impart;
   And there's rest for the weary worn traveler's feet,
   And joy for the sorrowing heart.   *Chorus.*

3 There is love in the valley of blessing so sweet,
   Such as none but the blood-washed may feel;
   When heaven comes down redeemed spirits to greet,
   And Christ sets his covenant seal.   *Chorus.*

4 There's a song in the valley of blessing so sweet,
   That angels would fain join the strain—
   As, with rapturous praises, we bow at his feet,
   Crying, "Worthy the Lamb that was slain!"   *Chorus.*

Alas! and did my Saviour bleed? 13

ISAAC WATTS, 1709. S. J. VAIL.

2 Was it for crimes that I have done
 He groaned upon the tree?
 Amazing pity! grace unknown!
 And love beyond degree! *Chorus.*

3 Well might the sun in darkness hide,
 And shut his glories in,
 When Christ, the mighty maker, died,
 For man, the creature's sin. *Chorus.*

4 Thus might I hide my blushing face
 While his dear cross appears;
 Dissolve my heart in thankfulness,
 And melt mine eyes to tears. *Chorus*

5 But drops of grief can ne'er repay
 The debt of love I owe:
 Here, Lord, I give myself away,—
 'Tis all that I can do. *Chorus.*

14. The Rifted Rock.

L. T. H.
Rev. R. LOWRY.
From "Pure Gold," by per.

2 Many a stormy sea I've traversed,
Many a tempest-shock have known;
Have been driven, without anchor,
On the barren shores, and lone.

Yet I now have found a haven,
Never moved by tempest-shock,
Where my soul is safe forever,
In the blessed Rifted Rock. Cho.

Welcome to Glory.   15

Words by Mrs. P. PALMER.   Mrs. J. F. KNAPP, by per.

2 When from Calvary's mount I rise,
   And pass through the portals above,
   Will shouts, Welcome home to the skies!
   Resound through the regions of love?
      Welcome home! etc.

3 Yes! loved ones who knew me below,
   Who learned the new song with me here,
   In chorus will hail me, I know,
   And welcome me home with good cheer!
      Welcome home! etc.

4 The beautiful gates will unfold,
   The home of the blood-washed I'll see;
   The city of saints I'll behold!
   For, O! there's a welcome for me!
      Welcome home! etc.

5 A sinner made whiter than snow,
   I'll join in the mighty acclaim,
   And shout through the gates as I go,
   Salvation to God and the Lamb!
      Welcome home! etc.

16 The Sweet By-and-By.

*By permission of OLIVER DITSON & CO.

Glory to the Lamb. 17

Rev. B. W. GORHAM, Arr.

1. The world is o-ver-come by the blood of the Lamb.
2. My sins are washed a-way, In the blood of the Lamb.

CHORUS.

Glory to the Lamb! Glory to the Lamb! Glory to the Lamb!

3 I've washed my garments white,
In the blood of the Lamb.
Glory to the Lamb, etc.

4 I've lost the fear of death
Through the blood of the Lamb.
Glory to the Lamb, etc.

5 The martyrs overcame
By the blood of the Lamb.
Glory to the Lamb, etc.

6 I soon shall gain the skies,
Through the blood of the Lamb.
Glory to the Lamb, etc.

Tune, "IN THE SWEET BY AND BY," page 16.

2.
We shall sing on that beautiful shore
The melodious songs of the blest,
And our spirits shall sorrow no more,
Not a sigh for the blessing of rest.
In the sweet, etc.

3.
To our bountiful Father above,
We will offer the tribute of praise,
For the glorious gift of his love,
And the blessings that hallow our days!
In the sweet, etc.

4.
We shall rest on that beautiful shore,
In the joys of the sav'd we shall share;
All our pilgrimage-toil will be o'er,
And the conquerors crown we shall wear. In the sweet, etc.

5.
We shall meet, we shall sing, we shall reign
In the land where the saved never die!
We shall rest free from sorrow and pain,
Safe at home in the sweet by-and by. In the sweet, etc.

18   I'm Kneeling at the Cross.

Words by Rev. J. PARKER.   Music by S. J. VAIL.

2 I rest, I rest supremely blest,
   Without a care to canker;
No gloomy night, my path is light,
   My hope holds like an anchor.
     And still I'm kneeling, etc.

3 My cup, my cup it runneth o'er,
   With joy celestial brimming;
On wings of love I soar above,
   His hallelujahs hymning.
     And still I'm kneeling, etc.

4 The blood, the blood is all my song,
   I have no bliss without it;
From every stain it makes me clean,
   My life and lip shall shout it.
     And still I'm kneeling, etc.

3 I rise to walk in heaven's own light,
Above the world and sin,
With heart made pure, and garments white,
And Christ enthron'd within. *Cho.*

4 Amazing grace! 'tis heaven below
To feel the blood applied;
And Jesus, only Jesus know,
My Jesus crucified. *Cho.*

20 The Cleansing Fountain.

COWPER, 1779.   Old Melody.

1. There is a fountain fill'd with blood, Drawn from Immanuel's veins;
And sinners plung'd beneath that flood, Lose all their guilt-y stains.

CHORUS.
Lose all their guilt-y stains, Lose all their guilt-y stains,
And sinners plung'd beneath that flood, Lose all their guilt-y stains.

2 The dying thief rejoiced to see
That fountain in his day;
And there may I, though vile as he,
Wash all my sins away.
          Cho. Wash all, etc.

3 Thou dying lamb! thy precious blood
Shall never lose its power,
Till all the ransom'd Church of God
Are saved to sin no more.
          Cho. Are saved, etc.

4 E'er since by faith I saw the stream
Thy flowing wounds supply,
Redeeming love has been my theme,
And shall be till I die.
          Cho. And shall, etc.

5 Then in a nobler, sweeter song,
I'll sing thy power to save,
When this poor lisping stamm'ring tongue
Lies silent in the grave.
          Cho. Lies silent, etc

Secret Prayer.   21

FANNY CROSBY.   W. H. DOANE.
From "Royal Diadem," by per.

2 When one by one, like threads of gold,
The hues of twilight fall,
O sweet communion with my God,
My Saviour and my all!

3 I hear seraphic tones that float
Amid celestial air,

And bathe my soul in streams of joy
Alone in secret prayer.

4 O when the hour of death shall come,
How sweet from thence to rise,
With prayer on earth my latest breath,
My watchword to the skies.

22. How Can I keep from Singing?

F. J. HARTLEY.
Rev. R. LOWRY.
From "Bright Jewels," by per.

1. My life flows on in endless song; Above earth's lam-en-ta-tion,
I catch the sweet, tho' far-off hymn That hails a new cre-a-tion;
Through all the tu-mult and the strife, I hear the mu-sic ring-ing;
It finds an ech-o in my soul—How can I keep from singing?

2 What though my joys and comfort die?
The Lord my Saviour liveth;
What though the darkness gather round?
Songs in the night he giveth,
No storm can shake my inmost calm,
While to that refuge clinging;
Since Christ is Lord of heaven and earth,
How can I keep from singing?

3 I lift my eyes; the cloud grows thin;
I see the blue above it;
And day by day this pathway smooths,
Since first I learned to love it;
The peace of Christ makes fresh my heart,
A fountain ever springing;
All things are mine since I am his—
How can I keep from singing?

We shall meet. 23

Rev. JOHN ATKINSON.
HUBERT P. MAIN, 1867.
From "Bright Jewels," by per.

1. We shall meet beyond the riv-er, By-and-by, by-and-by;
And the darkness shall be o-ver, By-and-by, by-and-by;
With the toil-some journey done, And the glorious bat-tle won,
We shall shine forth as the sun, By-and-by, by-and-by.

2. We shall strike the harps of glo-ry, By-and-by, by-and-by;
We shall sing redemption's sto-ry, By-and-by, by-and-by;
And the strains for-ev-er-more Shall re-sound in sweetness o'er
Yonder ev-er-last-ing shore, By-and-by, by-and-by.

3.
We shall see and be like Jesus,
By-and-by, by-and-by;
Who a crown of life will give us,
By-and-by, by-and-by;
And the angels who fulfil
All the mandates of His will,
Shall attend, and love us still,
By-and-by, by-and-by.

4.
There our tears shall all cease flow-
By-and-by, by-and-by; [ing,
And with sweetest rapture knowing,
By-and-by, by-and-by;
All the blest ones who have gone
To the land of life and song,
We with shoutings shall rejoin,
By-and by, by-and-by.

24   Oh, Sing of His Mighty Love.

Rev. F. BOTTOME. D. D.   Music by WM. B. BRADBURY, by per.

2 Oh, bliss of the purified! Jesus is mine,
No longer in dread condemnation I pine;
In conscious salvation I sing of his grace,
Who lifted upon me the smiles of his face!—*Cho.*

3 Oh, bliss of the purified! bliss of the pure!
No wound hath the soul that his blood cannot cure;
No sorrow-bowed head but may sweetly find rest,—
No tears but may dry them on Jesus' breast. *Cho.*

4 O Jesus the Crucified! thee will I sing!
My blessed Redeemer! my God and my King!
My soul filled with rapture shall shout o'er the grave,
And triumph at death, in the MIGHTY TO SAVE. *Cho.*

Whiter than Snow. 25

JAMES NICHOLSON. Wm. G. FISCHER, by per.

2 Dear Jesus, come down from thy throne in the skies,
And help me to make a complete sacrifice;
I give up myself, and whatever I know—
Now wash me, and I shall be whiter than snow.
CHO.—Whiter than snow, &c.

3 Dear Jesus, for this I most humbly entreat;
I wait, blessed Lord, at thy crucified feet,
By faith, for my cleansing, I see thy blood flow—
Now wash me, and I shall be whiter than snow.
CHO.—Whiter than snow, &c.

4 The blessing by faith, I receive from above;
O glory! my soul is made perfect in love;
My prayer has prevailed, and this moment I know,
The blood is applied, I am whiter than snow.
CHO.—Whiter than snow, &c.

26. Our Loved Ones gone before.

2 Hark the words of our Master, be faithful, watch and pray,
  Press on where joys eternal flow ;
  Let us journey together along the shining way,
  And sing rejoicing as we go. *Cho.*

3 We are pilgrims to Zion, though trials we must bear.
  We'll count them blessings in disguise;
  Though the cross may be heavy, the crown we soon shall wear,
  In heaven, where pleasure never dies. *Cho.*

SORROW SHALL COME AGAIN NO MORE.

1 What to me are earth's pleasures, and what its flowing tears ?
  What are all the sorrows I deplore ?
  There's a song ever swelling, still lingers on my ears,
  "Oh, sorrow shall come again no more."
  Cho.—'T is a song from the home of the weary:
    " Sorrow, sorrow is for ever o'er:
      Happy now, ever happy, on Canaan's peaceful shore.
      Oh, sorrow shall come again no more."

Words and Melody by
Rev. DWIGHT WILLIAMS.

Harmonized by
S. J. VAIL.

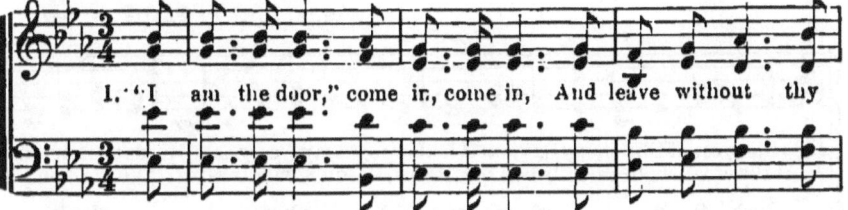

2 "I am the door,"
    Come, gently knock,
And I will loose the heavy lock,
That guards my Father's precious fold;
Come in from darkness and from cold.

3 "I am the door,"
    No longer roam,
Here are thy treasures, here thy home;
I purchased them for thee and thine,
And paid the price in blood divine.

4 "I am the door,"
    My Father waits
To make thee heir of rich estates;
Come, dwell with him, and dwell with me,
And thou my Father's child shall be.

5 "I am the door,"
    Come in, come in,
And everlasting treasures win;
My Father's house was built for thee,
And thou shalt share his home with me.

---

2 I seek not earthly glory, nor mingle with the gay;
   I desire not this world's gilded store:
   There are voices now calling from those bright realms of day,
   "Oh, sorrow shall come again no more." *Cho.*

3 'Tis a note that is wafted across the troubled wave;
   'Tis a song I've heard upon the shore;
   T is a sweet-thrilling murmur around the Christian's grave:
   "Oh, sorrow shall come again no more."—*Cho.*

(Tune page 26.)

28. Resting at the Cross.

WM. J. KIRKPATRICK, by per.

1. To the cross of Christ, my Saviour, I had brought my weary soul, Burden'd, faint, and broken hearted, Praying, "Jesus make me whole."
2. At the cross, while meekly bowing, Jesus, smiling, bade me live; "I have died for your transgressions, And I freely all forgive."

CHORUS.

Glory, glory be to Jesus, I am counting all but dross; I have found a full salvation, I am resting at the cross; I'm resting at the cross, I'm resting at the cross, I'm resting at the cross.

3 At the cross, while prostrate lying,
  Jesus' blood flowed o'er my soul,
  All my guilt and sin were covered,
  And He whispered, "Child be whole."
  Cho.

4 At the cross, I'm calmly trusting,
  Every moment now is sweet;
  I am tasting of His glory,
  I am resting at His feet. Cho.

O Thou God of my Salvation. 29

Rev. CHAS. WESLEY.   C. C. CONVERSE, by per.

1. O thou God of my salvation, My Redeemer from all sin; Moved by thy divine compassion, Who hast died my heart to win, I will praise thee: I will praise thee: Where shall I thy praise begin?
I will praise thee: I will praise thee: Where shall I thy praise begin.

2 Tho' unseen, I love the Saviour;
He hath brought salvation near;
Manifests his pard'ning favor;
And when Jesus doth appear,
||: Soul and body :||
Shall his glorious image bear.

3 While the angel choirs are crying,—
Glory to the great I Am,
I with them will still be vying—
Glory! glory to the Lamb!
||: O how precious :||
Is the sound of Jesus' name!

4 Angels now are hov'ring round us,
Unperceived amid the throng;
Wond'ring at the love that crown'd us,
Glad to join the holy song: [us,
||: Hallelujah, :||
Love and praise to Christ belong!

30. For Thou hast died for Me.

Words by FANNY CROSBY, July, 1866.
Wm. B. BRADBURY.
From " Trio," by per.

1. When clouds hang darkly o'er my way And earthly comfort dies, On thee my Saviour and my God, My every hope relies. I hear thy spirits gentle voice, Thy cross by faith I see, Thy precious blood O, dying Lamb! Redeems and makes me what I am, For thou hast died for me, For thou hast died for me.

2 My soul, confiding in thy word,
  Can rest securely there,
And feel at peace in every storm,
  Beneath thy watchful care ;
A sinner lost, but saved by grace
  Be this my only plea :
Thy precious blood, O dying Lamb
Redeems and makes me what I am
  For thou hast died for me.

3 O when I leave this mortal scene,
  And rise to worlds of light ;
Then shall I see thee as thou art,
  Arrayed in glory bright :
There by the living stream divine,
  My raptured song shall be ;
Thy precious blood, O dying Lamb'
Redeems and makes me what I am,
  For thou hast died for me.

My Ain Countrie.   31

Miss M. A. LEE.   Scotch Song. Arr.

2 I've his gude word of promise. that some gladsome day the King,
To his ain royal palace, his banished hame, will bring
Wi'een, an' wi' heart running owre we shall see
"The King in his beauty," an' our ain countrie,
My sins hae been mony, and my sorrows hae been sair;
But there they'll never vex me, nor be remembered mair.
For his bluid hath made me white, and his hand shall dry my e'e,
When he brings me hame at last to my ain countrie.

3 Like a bairn to its mither, a wee birdie to its nest,
I wad fain be ganging noo unto my Saviour's breast,
For he gathers in his bosom witless worthless lambs like me,
An' "he carries them himsel'," to his ain countrie.
He's faithfu' that hath promised, he'll surely come again,
He'll keep his tryst wi' me, at what hour I dinna ken;
But he bids me still to wait, an' ready aye to be,
To gang at ony moment to my ain countrie.

4 So I'm watching aye, and singing o'my hame as I wait,
For the soun'ing o' his footfa' this side the gowden gate,
God gie his grace to ilk ane wha listens noo to me,
That we may a'gaug in gladness to our ain countrie.

[Last four lines of 1st verse can be sung to complete 4th verse.]

By the Gate they'll meet us. 33

Mrs. LYDIA BAXTER.
HUBERT P. MAIN, 1872.
From "Royal Diadem," by per.

1. In the fadeless spring-time, on the heav'nly shore, Kindred spirits wait us, who have gone be-fore; There no flow-ers with-er, and no pleasures cloy, In that land of beau-ty, In that home of joy. By the gate they'll meet us, 'neath that golden sky, Meet us at the por-tal—Meet us by-and-by.

2 In the misty gloaming, death awaits us all;
Silent is his coming, sure the Master's call;
And the angel-footsteps mark the upward way,
Till the twilight merges into heavenly day.—*Cho.*

3 Trusting in the Saviour, may we humbly wait,
Till the holy angels ope the pearly gate;
And the loving Father, from His gracious throne,
Smiling bids us welcome to our heavenly home.—*Cho.*

34   Under His Wings.

JAMES NICHOLSON.   ASA HULL, by per.

1. In God I have found a re-treat, Where I can se-cure-ly a-bide; No refuge, nor rest so com-plete, And here I in-tend to re-side.

CHORUS. Oh, what comfort it brings, As my soul sweetly sings: I am safe from all dan-ger While un-der his wings.

2 I dread not the terror by night,
   No arrow can harm me by day;
   His shadow has covered me quite,
   My fears He has driven away. *Cho.*

3 The pestilence walking about,
   When darkness has settled abroad,
   Can never compel me to doubt
     The presence and power of God. *Cho.*

4 The wasting destruction at noon,
   No fearful foreboding can bring;
   With Jesus, my soul doth commune,
   His perfect salvation I sing. *Cho.*

5 A thousand may fall at my side,
   And ten thousand at my right hand;
   Above me His wings are spread wide,
   Beneath them in safety I stand. *Cho.*

Only one Way to the Cross. 35

Words by Rev. JOHN PARKER. S. J. VAIL, by per.

3 There is only one cross to be borne,
 That cross is not heavy to bear,
 It may call thee in conflict and scorn,
 ||: To confess Him—His burdens to share. :|| *Refr.*

4 There is only one kingdom to win,
 One home with the blood-washed above;
 He'll help thee who died for thy sin;
 ||: Oh, fear not, but trust in His love. :|| *Refr.*

36. The River of Song.

FANNY CROSBY. 1873. Wm. H. DOANE.
From "Royal Diadem," by per.

1. O the sleep of just a moment, When the spir-it sinks a-way!
2. We shall hear ce-les-tial mu-sic O'er its bosom sweep a-long,

Then the waking, blissful wak-ing, In a world of endless day!
Like the voice of many wa-ters; Hark! the ev-er-last-ing song.

CHORUS.

O the rap-ture, ho-ly rap-ture, There to stand with the bright happy
O the rapture there, ho-ly rapture there,

throng! There the sacred springs of pleasure with the streams of love unite, In a

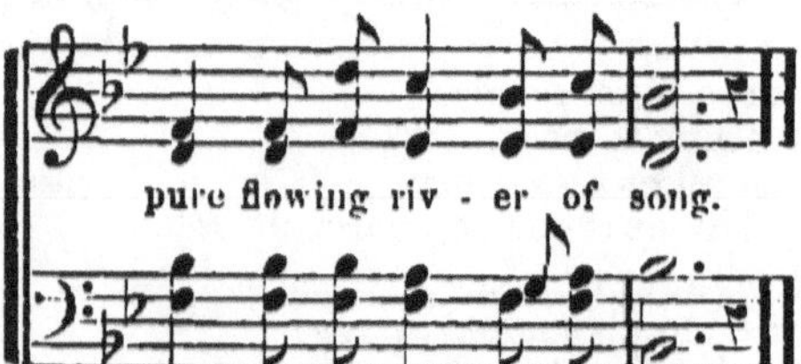

pure flowing riv-er of song.

3.
Worthy is the Lamb forever,
Worthy is the Lamb, they cry
Glory, glory, hallelujah,
Glory be to God on high!
O the rapture, &c.

38. Light and Comfort.

FANNY J. CROSBY. 1867. Wm. B. BRADBURY, by per.

1. Light and com-fort of my soul, When the bil-lows o'er me roll,
2. Lord, my soul in tears would mourn, All the anguish Thou hast borne,
3. Mocked and scourged—condemned to die, On the cross extend-ed high,

Thou dest bid me in Thy word Cast my bur-den on the Lord,
In the gar-den I would be, Lone-ly watch-er still with Thee.
Ten-ant of the lone-ly tomb, Might-y conqu'ror o'er its gloom,

Je-sus, Sav-iour once betray'd, Sac-ri-fice for sin-ners made;
Thou hast suffer'd Thou hast bled, Thorns have pierc'd Thy sacred head;
Crowned victo-rious God of love, To thy Father's home a-bove,

Wretched, lost, to Thee I fly, Save, O save me, or I die.
Je-sus, while I cling to thee, Let Thy sor-row plead for me.
Grant my soul a place, at last, Where the storms of life are past.

2 O, think of the friends over there,
Who before us the journey have trod,
Of the songs that they breathe on the air,
In their home in the palace of God.
Over there, over there,
O think of the friends over there

3 I'll soon be at home over there,
For the end of my journey I see;
Many dear to my heart over there,
Are watching and waiting for me.
Over there, over there,
I'll soon be at home over there.

40. Jesus paid it all.

PROCTOR.
WM. B. BRADBURY, by per.

1 Naught of merit or of price,
  Remains to justice due ;
  Jesus died, and paid it all,—
  Yes, all the debt I owe.

Cho.—Jesus paid it all,
  All the debt I owe,
  Jesus died and paid it all,
  Yes, all the debt I owe.

2 When he from his lofty throne,
  Stoop'd down to do and die,
  Every thing was fully done ;
  "'Tis finished!" was his cry,—*Cho.*

3 Weary not, O toiling one,
  Whate'er thy conflict be.
  Work for him with cheerful heart,
  Who suffered all for thee.—*Cho.*

4 Clinging to the Saviour's cross,
  Look up by simple faith,
  Praise him for the pard'ning love
  That saves from endless death.—*Cho.*

5 Bring a willing sacrifice—
  Thy soul to Jesus' feet ;
  Stand in him, in him alone,
  All glorious and complete.—*Cho.*

Shall we meet in Heaven. 41

1 Shall we meet in heaven, shall we meet in heaven,
  With the blest who have gone before?
  Will a crown be given, will a crown be given,
  When we stand on the other shore? *Refr.*

2 Will the angels bright, will the angels bright,
  Bear us on to that happy home?
  With the saints in light, with the saints in light,
  Shall we stand round the great white throne? *Refr.*

3 Yes, we all may meet, yes, we all may meet,
  Where this life and its toils are o'er,
  And each other greet, and each other greet,
  In a land where we'll part no more. *Refr.*

42. Wondrous Love.

Mrs. M. STOCKTON. Wm. G. FISCHER, by per.

1.
God lov'd the world of sinners lost,
　And ruin'd by the fall ;
Salvation full at highest cost,
　He offers free to all. *Cho.*

2.
E'en now by faith I claim Him mine,
　The risen Son of God ;
Redemption by his death I find,
　And cleansing through His blood.
　　　　　　　　　Cho.

3.
Love brings the glorious fullness in,
　And to his saints makes known ;
The blessed rest from inbred sin,
　Through faith in Christ alone.
　　　　　　　　　Cho.

4.
Believing souls rejoicing go,
　There shall to you be given,
A glorious foretaste here below
　Of endless life in heaven. *Cho.*

5.
Of victory now o'er Satan's power,
　Let all the ransom'd sing
And triumph in the dying hour,
　Thro' Christ, the Lord, our King.
　　　　　　　　　Cho.

Rest in Thee.

43

E. TURNEY, D. D.

Rev. R. LOWRY, by per.
From "Royal Diadem."

1. Blessed Jesus, Blessed Jesus, Thou who gav'st thyself for me,
2. Hope of all the meek and lowly, Thou my hope and joy shalt be:

Leave me not in sin to wander; Bid me come and rest in Thee.
Blessed Jesus, Blessed Jesus, Bid me come and rest in Thee.

REFRAIN.

Rest in Thee, Rest in Thee, Bid me come and rest in Thee;
Rest in Thee, Rest in Thee, Bid me come and rest in Thee.

3 Draw me from each sinful striving;
From myself, O set me free:
Blessed Jesus, Blessed Jesus,
Bid me come and rest in Thee.
Refr.

4 Highest, purest, sweetest pleasure,
Shall thy service bring to me:
Blessed Jesus, Blessed Jesus,
Bid me come and rest in Thee.
Refr.

44. Beautiful Home of the Blest.

Words and Music by W. BENNETT. From "Royal Diadem." by per.

2 Home by the river of life,
  Beautiful home, beautiful home!
  Free from earth's passion and strife,
  Beautiful home on high!
  Home where the pris'ner finds sweet release;
  Home where all sorrows forever cease;
  Home where the ransom'd ones dwell in peace,
  Happy forever there. *Cho.*

3 Home of the glorified throng,
  Beautiful home, beautiful home!
  Home of the shout and the song,
  Beautiful home on high!
  Home where the beautiful angels dwell;

Home of the blessed, where all is well;
Home of sweet raptures no tongue can tell,
Ever increasing there. *Cho.*

4 Home in the city of gold,
  Beautiful home, beautiful home!
  Home where are pleasures untold,
  Beautiful home on high!
  Home where the many bright mansions be;
  Home where the children their Saviour see;
  Home where they worship eternally,
  Praising him ever there. *Cho.*

The Penitent. 45

Rev. JOHN G. CHAFEE.
CHESTER G. ALLEN, by per.
From "Bright Jewels."

1. Can my soul find rest from sorrow, Can my sins forgiven be,
Must I wait until tomorrow Ere my Saviour speaks to me?
Will He speak in words of kindness? Will He wash away my sin?
Will He lift this vale of blindness, And remove this deadly pain?

2 O, the darkness, how it thickens,
   Like the brooding of despair!
And my soul within me sickens—
   God, in mercy, hear my prayer!
Give me but a hope to cherish.
   Give me just one ray of light—
Help me, save me, or I perish,
   Take away this awful night!

3 Now He hears me, He will save me,
   I behold His shining face,
Hear Him whisper He will have me—
   O, the miracle of grace!
I will joy to tell the story
   How He cometh from above—
Fills my soul, O glory, glory!
   With the blessings of His love

46. Save me at the Cross

*FANNY J. CROSBY, 1874. Arr. by H. P. MAIN.

1. { Lov-ing Saviour, hear my cry, hear my cry, hear my cry,
   { I have sinn'd but Thou hast died, Thou hast died, Thou hast died,
   Trembling to Thy arms I fly, O save me at the cross:
   In Thy mer-cy let me bide, O save me at the cross.

CHORUS.
Dear Jesus re-ceive me, No more would I grieve Thee,
Now, bless-ed Re-deem-er, O save me at the cross.

2 Though I perish, ‖ I will pray, ‖
Thou of life the living way,
   O save me at the cross.
Thou hast said-Thy ‖ grace is free, ‖
Have compassion, Lord, on me,
   O save me at the cross.
      Dear Jesus, etc.

3 Wash me in Thy ‖ cleansing blood. ‖
Plunge me now beneath the flood,
   O save me at the cross.
Only faith will ‖ pardon bring, ‖
In that faith to Thee I cling,
   O save me at the cross.
      Dear Jesus, etc.

* Entered according to Act of Congress, A.D. 1874, by Biglow & Main, in the Office of the Librarian of Congress, at Washington.

I come to Thee! 47

FANNY J. CROSBY, 1868.   SYLVESTER MAIN, 1868.

1. I come to thee, I come to thee! Thou precious Lamb who died for me, I rest con-fid-ing in thy word, And "cast my bur-den on the Lord." I come to thee with all my grief, Dear Saviour, help my un-be-lief; Thy blessed name, my on-ly plea, With this, O Lord, I come to thee!

2 I come to thee, whose sovereign power
Can cheer me in the darkest hour,
I come to thee, thro' storm and shade—
For thou hast said, " be not afraid."
I come to thee with all my tears,
My pain and sorrow, doubt and fears;
Thou precious Lamb, who died for me,
I come to thee, I come to thee!

3 To thee my trembling spirit flies,
When faith grows weak, and comfort dies
I bow adoring at thy feet,
And hold with thee communion sweet—
O wondrous love! O joy divine!
To feel thee near and call thee mine!
Thou precious Lamb, who died for me,
I come to thee, I come to thee!

48 All to Christ I Owe.

Mrs. E. M. HALL. J. T. GRAPE.

2.
Lord, now indeed I find
  Thy faith, and thine alone,
Can change the leper's spots,
  And melt the heart of stone. *Cho.*

3.
For nothing good have I
  Whereby thy grace to claim—
I'll wash my garment white
  In the blood of Calv'ry's Lamb.
      Cho.

4.
When from my dying bed
  My ransomed soul shall rise,
Then "Jesus paid it all"
  Shall rend the vaulted skies. *Cho.*

5.
And when before the throne
  I stand in him complete,
I'll lay my trophies down,
  All down at Jesus' feet. *Cho.*

The Song of Hope.　49

S. J. VAIL, by per.

2 I hear hope singing sweetly singing,
　Softly in an under tone ;
　And singing as if God had taught it,
　||: "It is better farther on." :||

3 By night and day it sings the same song,—
　Sings it while I sit alone :
　And sings it so the heart may hear it,
　||: "It is better farther on." :||

4 It sits upon the grave and sings it—
　Sings it when the heart would groan ;
　And sings it when the shadows darken,
　||; "It is better farther on." :||

5 Still farther on ! O how much farther ?
　Count the mile stones one by one ;
　No ! no ! no counting—only trusting,
　||: "It is better farther on." :||

The Bright Forever. Concluded. 51

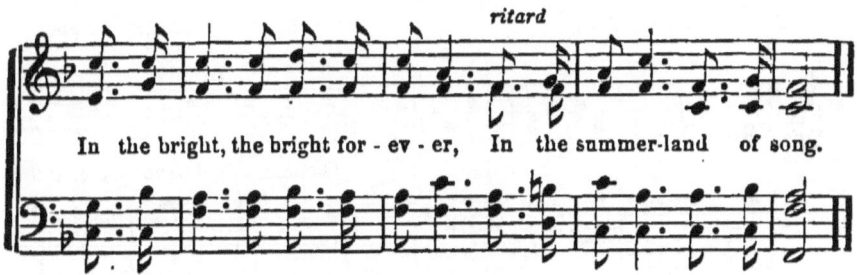

In the bright, the bright for-ev-er, In the summer-land of song.

2.
Yet a little while we linger,
 Ere we reach our journey's end;
Yet a little while to labor,
 Ere the evening shades descend,
Then we'll lay us down to slumber,
 But the night will soon be o'er;
In the bright, the bright forever,
 We shall wake to sleep no more.
   Cho.

3.
O the bliss of life eternal!
 O the long unbroken rest!
In the golden fields of pleasure,
 In the region of the blest.
But, to see our dear Redeemer,
 And before His throne to fall,
There to hear His gracious welcome
 Will be sweeter far than all.
   Cho.

Come, Come to Jesus!

Rev. Geo. B. PECK.   HUBERT P. MAIN, by per.

1 Come, come to Jesus!
  He waits to welcome thee,
  O Wand'rer, eagerly;
  Come, come to Jesus!

2 Come, come to Jesus!
  He waits to ransom thee,
  O Slave! eternally;
  Come, come to Jesus!

3 Come, come to Jesus!
  He waits to lighten thee,
  O Burdened! trustingly;
  Come, come to Jesus!

4 Come, come to Jesus!
  He waits to give to thee.
  O Blind! a vision free;
  Come, come to Jesus!

5 Come, come to Jesus!
  He waits to shelter thee,
  O Weary! blessedly;
  Come, come to Jesus!

6 Come, come to Jesus!
  He waits to carry thee.
  O Lamb! so lovingly;
  Come, come to Jesus!

52 The Land of Beulah. C. M.

Rev. J. HASKELL. Wm. B. BRADBURY, by per.

[Music: O come, angel band, come, and around me stand, O bear me away on your snowy wings, To my immortal home, O bear me away on your snowy wings, To my immortal home.]

1 My latest sun is sinking fast,
 My race is nearly run;
 My strongest trials now are past,
 My triumph is begun. *Refr.*

2 I know I'm nearing the holy ranks,
 Of friends and kindred dear,
 For I brush the dews on Jordan's banks,
 The crossing must be near.—*Refr.*

3 I've almost gained my heavenly home,
 My spirit loudly sings;
 The holy ones, behold they come!
 I hear the noise of wings,—*Refr.*

4 O, bear my longing heart to Him
 Who bled and died for me;
 Whose blood now cleanses from all sin,
 And gives me victory.—*Refr.*

I am trusting, Lord, in Thee. 53

Words by Rev. Wm. Mc DONALD.   Wm. G. FISCHER, by per.

Cho. I am trusting, Lord in thee, Dear Lamb of Calvary ; Save me, Jesus, save me now
Humbly at thy cross I bow ;

1 I am coming to the cross ;
I am poor and weak and blind ;
I am counting all but dross ;
I shall full salvation find. *Cho.*

2 Long my heart has sigh'd for thee;
Long has evil reigned within ;
Jesus sweetly speaks to me,
I will cleanse you from all sin. *Cho.*

3 Here I give my all to thee,—
Friends, and time, and earthly store;

Soul and body thine to be—
Wholly thine—forever more. *Cho.*

4 In the promises I trust ;
Now I feel the blood applied ;
I am prostrate in the dust ;
I with Christ am crucified. *Cho.*

5 Jesus comes ! he fills my soul !
Perfected in love I am ;
I am every whit made whole ;
Glory, glory to the Lamb. *Cho.*

The Resurrection. 8s.

Rev. WM. B. COLLIER.   FINE.

1. { The angels that watch'd round the tomb Where low the Redeemer was laid. }
   { When deep in mor-tal - i- ty's gloom, He hid, for a sea-son his head. }
D. C. Have witness'd his rising, and swept Their chords with the triumphs of joy.

That veil'd their fair forms while he slept, And ceas'd their sweet harps to employ,

2 Ye saints, who once languished below,
But long since have entered your rest,
I pant to be glorified too,
And lean on Immanuel's breast ;
The grave in which Jesus was laid
Hath buried my guilt and my fears ;
And while I contemplate its shade,
The light of his presence appears.

3 O! sweet is the season of rest
When life's weary journey is done ;
The blush that spreads over its west,
The last ling'ring rays of its sun.
Though dreary the empire of night,

I soon shall emerge from its gloom,
And see immortality's light
Arise on the shades of the tomb.

4 Then, welcome the last rending sighs,
When these aching heart-strings shall break,
And death shall extinguish these eyes,
And moisten with dew the pale cheek ;
No terror the prospect begets ;
I am not mortality's slave ;
The sunbeam of life as it sets
Leaves a halo of peace round the grave.

54. Sweet Rest in Heaven.

Wm. B. BRADBURY, by per.

1.
Come, brethren, don't grow weary,
  But let us journey on :
The passing scenes all tell us
  That death will surely come ;
The moments will not tarry ;
  This life will soon be gone :
These bodies soon will moulder
  In th' dark and weary tomb : *Cho.*

2.
Loved ones have gone before us,
  They beckon us away,
O'er aerial plains they're soaring,
  Blest in eternal day ;
But we are in the army,
  And dare not leave our post ;
We'll fight until we conquer
  The foes' most mighty host. *Cho.*

3 Our Captain's gone before us,
  He kindly calls us home
To yonder world of glory,
  And sweetly bids us come,
The world, the flesh, and Satan,
  Will strive to hedge our way,
But we'll o'ercome these powers,
  If we hourly watch and pray. *Cho.*

3. One more day's work for Jesus;
  How sweet the work has been,
  To tell the story,
  To show the glory,
  Where Christ's flock enter in!
  How it did shine
  In this poor heart of mine! *Cho.*

4. One more day's work for Jesus—
  O, yes, a weary day;
  But heaven shines clearer
  And rest comes nearer,
  At each step of the way;
  And Christ in all—
  Before his face I fall. *Cho.*

5. O, blessed work for Jesus!
  O, rest at Jesus' feet!
  There toil seems pleasure,
  My wants are treasure,
  And pain for Him is sweet,
  Lord, if I may,
  I'll serve another day! *Cho.*

56 "The Sinner invited." 6s & 7s.

Rev. C. B. DAVIDSON.   Arr. by Rev. W. McDONALD.

1.
Sinner, come will you go!
  To the highlands of heaven?
Where the storms never blow,
  And the long summer's given:
Where the bright blooming flow'rs,
  Are their odors emitting;
And the leaves of the bow'rs.
  In the breezes are flitting.

2.
Where the saints robed in white—
  Cleansed in life's flowing fountain;
Shining beauteous and bright,
  They inhabit the mountain,

Where no sin, nor dismay,
  Neither trouble, nor sorrow,
Will be felt for a day,
  Nor be feared for the morrow.

3.
He's prepared thee a home—
  Sinner, canst thou believe it?
And invites thee to come—
  Sinner, wilt thou receive it?
O come, sinner, come!
  For the tide is receding,
And the Saviour will soon
  And forever cease pleading.

I am Thine Own.

Mrs HELEN BRADLEY.   Rev. A. A. WRIGHT.

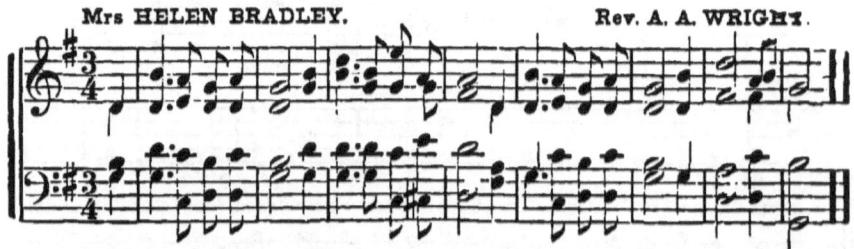

1 I am thine own, O Christ;
    Henceforth entirely thine;
  And life from this glad hour,
    New life is mine.

2 No earthly joy can lure
    My quiet soul from thee:
  This deep delight so pure,
    Is heaven to me.

3 My joyful song of praise
    In sweet content I sing;
  To Thee the note I raise,
    My King! My King!

4 I cannot tell the art
    By which such bliss is given:
  I know thou hast my heart,
    And I—have heaven.

5 O peace,—O holy rest,
    O balmy breath of love:
  O heart, divinest, best,—
    Thy depth I prove.

6 I ask this gift of Thee—
    A life all lily fair,
  And fragrant as the place
    Where seraphs are!

Revive us again. 57

Rev. W. P. MACKEY. From "New Praises of Jesus," by per.

Halle-lu-jah! Thine the glory, Halle-lujah! Amen.
Halle-lu-jah! Thine the glory, [OMIT............ Revive us a-gain

1 We praise Thee O God! for the Son of Thy love,
For Jesus, who died, and is now gone above. *Cho.*

2 We praise Thee, O God! for Thy Spirit of light,
Who has shown us our Saviour, and scattered our night. *Cho.*

3 All glory and praise to the Lamb that was slain,
Who has borne all our sins, and has cleansed every stain. *Cho.*

Who'll stand up for Jesus? 7s & 6s.

Words by Rev. L. H. Music by Rev. L. HARTSOUGH.

1. O who'll stand up for Je-sus, The lowly Naz-a-rene?
And raise the blood stain'd banner Amid the [OMIT.....] hosts of sin?
D.C. All hail reproach or sorrow If Je-sus [OMIT.....] leads me there.

CHORUS. D. C.

The Cross for Christ I'll cher-ish, Its cru-ci-fix-ion bear;

2 O who will follow Jesus,
  Amid reproach and shame?
Where others shrink or falter,
  Who'll glory in his name?

3 My all to Christ I've given,
  My talents, time, and voice,

Myself, my reputation,
  The lone way is my choice.

4 O Jesus, Jesus, Jesus,
  My all-sufficient Friend!
Come, fold me to thy bosom,
  E'en to the journey's end.

58 Home of the Soul.

Mrs. E. H. GATES. PHILIP PHILLIPS, by per.

The Lord will Provide. 59
C. S. HARRINGTON. by per. E. TOURJÉE.

Mrs. M. A. W. COOK.

2 Oh, that home of the soul in my visions and dreams,
  Its bright jasper walls I can see;
  Till I fancy but thinly the vail intervenes
  ||: Between the fair city and me. :||
                        Till I fancy, etc.
3 That unchangable home is for you and for me,
  Where Jesus of Nazareth stands;
  The King of all kingdoms forever is he,
  ||: And he holdeth our crowns in his hands. :||
                        The King of, etc.
4 Oh, how sweet it will be in that beautiful land,
  So free from all sorrow and pain;
  With songs on our lips and with harps in our hands
  ||: To meet one another again. :||
                        With songs on, etc.

Tune "Home of the Soul," on page 58.

Guide. 7s Double.

(1858.) Words and Music by M. M. WELLS.

1.
Holy Spirit, faithful guide,
Ever near the Christian's side;
Gently lead us by the hand,
Pilgrims in a desert land;
Weary souls for e'er rejoice,
While they hear that sweetest voice,
Whisp'ring softly, wanderer come!
Follow me, I'll guide thee home,

2.
Ever present, truest Friend,
Ever near thine aid to lend,
Leave us not to doubt and fear,
Groping on in darkness drear,
When the storms are raging sore,
Hearts grow faint, and hopes give o'er,
Whisp'ring softly, wanderer come!
Follow me, I'll guide thee home.

3.
When our days of toil shall cease,
Waiting still for sweet release,
Nothing left but heaven and prayer,
Wond'ring if our names were there;
Wading deep the dismal flood,
Pleading nought but Jesus' blood;
Whispering softly, wanderer, come!
Follow me, I'll guide thee home!

WHY WILL YE DIE?

1.
Sinners, turn; why will ye die?
God, your Maker, asks you why?
God, who did your being give,
Made you with himself to live;
He the fatal cause demands;
Asks the work of his own hands,—
Why, ye thankless creatures, why
Will ye cross his love, and die?

2.
Sinners, turn; why will ye die?
God, your Saviour, asks you why?
He, who did your souls retrieve,
Died himself, that you might live,
Will ye let him die in vain?
Crucify your Lord again?
Why, ye ransom'd sinners, why
Will ye slight his grace, and die?

C. WESLEY. 1756.

62. I'm going Home.

Rev. Wm. HUNTER.   *Dr. Wm. MILLER. Arr.*

1. My heavenly home is bright and fair: Nor pain, nor death can enter there:
Its glitt'ring towers the sun outshine, That heavenly mansion shall be mine.

CHORUS.

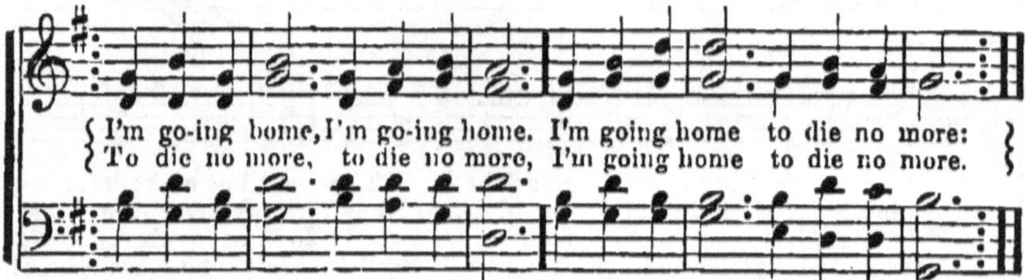

I'm go-ing home, I'm go-ing home. I'm going home to die no more:
To die no more, to die no more, I'm going home to die no more.

2 My Father's house is built on high,
Far, far above the starry sky ;
When from this earthly prison free,
That heavenly mansion mine shall be.
   I'm going home, etc.

3 While here a stranger, far from home,
Affliction's waves may round me foam ;
And though like Lazarus, sick and poor,
My heavenly mansion is secure.
   I'm going home, etc.

4 Let others seek a home below,
Which flames devour, or waves o'erflow;
Be mine the happier lot to own,
A heavenly mansion near the throne.
   I'm going home, etc.

5 Then fail this earth, let stars decline,
And sun and moon refuse to shine,
All nature sink, and cease to be,
That heavenly mansion stands for me.
   I'm going home, etc.

My Saviour, my almighty Friend.

A Freedmen's Melody.   *Harmonized by S. J. VAIL.*

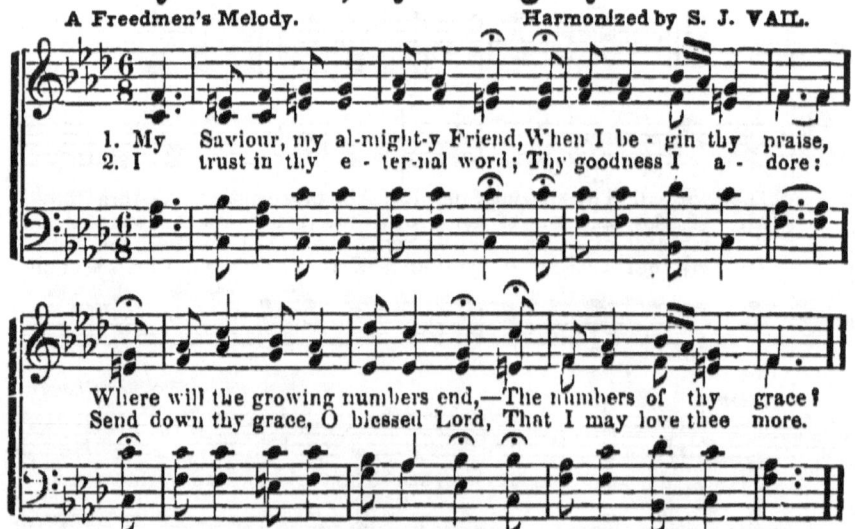

1. My Saviour, my al-might-y Friend, When I be-gin thy praise,
Where will the growing numbers end,—The numbers of thy grace?

2. I trust in thy e-ter-nal word; Thy goodness I a-dore:
Send down thy grace, O blessed Lord, That I may love thee more.

All for Jesus. 63

Words by MARY D. JAMES.　For Male Voices.　ASA HULL, by per.

1. All for Jesus! all for Je-sus! All my being's ransom'd pow'rs;
All my tho'ts and words and doings, All my days and all my hours.
All for Jesus: All for Jesus; All my days and all my hours.

2.
Let my hands perform his bidding;
Let my feet run in his ways;
Let my eyes see Jesus only;
Let my lips speak forth his praise.
All for Jesus! all for Jesus!
Let my lips speak forth his praise.

3.
Worldlings prize their gems of beauty
Cling to gilded toys of dust,
Boast of wealth, & fame, & pleasure;
Only Jesus will I trust.
Only Jesus! only Jesus!
Only Jesus will I trust.

4.
Since my eyes were fixed on Jesus,
I've lost sight of all beside,—
So enchained my spirit's vision,
Looking at the crucified.
All for Jesus! all for Jesus!
All for Jesus crucified!

5.
Oh, what wonder! how amazing!
Jesus, glorious King of kings,
Deigns to call me his beloved,
Let me rest beneath his wings.
All for Jesus! all for Jesus!
Resting now beneath his wings.

3.
My feet shall travel all the length
Of the celestial road; [strength,
And march with courage in thy
To see the Lord my God.

4.
Awake! awake! my tuneful powers,
With this delightful song;
And entertain the darkest hours,
Nor think the season long.

Tune, "MY SAVIOUR," etc., page 62.

64. Wrestling Jacob.

C. WESLEY, 1742. Arr. by Rev. W. Mc DONALD.

2 I need not tell thee who I am,
My sin and misery declare;
Thyself hast call'd me by my name;
Look on my hands, and read it there!
But who, I ask thee, who art thou?
Tell me thy name, and tell me now.

3 In vain thou strugglest to get free;
I never will unloose my hold:
Art thou the Man that died for me?
The secret of thy love unfold.
Wrestling, I will not let thee go,
Till I thy name, thy nature know.

4 Wilt thou not yet to me reveal
Thy new, unutterable name?
Tell me, I still beseech thee, tell;
To know it now resolved I am:
Wrestling, I will not let thee go,
Till I thy name, thy nature know.

5 What, though my shrinking flesh complain,
And murmur to contend so long?
I rise superior to my pain:
When I am weak, then I am strong:
And when my all of strength shall fail,
I shall with the God-man prevail.

The Cross. 65

I. WATTS. 1709. Rev. G. O. WELLS, Arr.

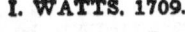

1 When I survey the wondrous cross
　On which the Prince of glory died,
　My richest gain I count but loss,
　　And pour contempt on all my pride.
CHORUS. The cross, the cross, the precious cross,
　　The wondrous cross of Jesus,
　　From all our sin, its guilt and pow'r,
　　And ev'ry stain, it frees us.
　　Then I'm clinging, clinging, clinging,
　　O, I'm clinging to the cross,
　　Yes, I'm clinging, clinging, clinging,
　　Clinging to the cross.

2 Forbid it, Lord, that I should boast,
　　Save in the death of Christ, my God;
　All the vain things that charm me most,
　　I sacrifice them to his blood. *Cho.*

3 See, from his head, his hands, his feet,
　　Sorrow and love flow mingled down:
　Did e'er such love and sorrow meet,
　　Or thorns compose so rich a crown? *Cho.*

4 Were the whole realm of nature mine,
　　That were a present far too small;
　Love so amazing, so divine,
　　Demands my soul, my life, my all. *Cho.*

　　✶ Use hold in repeat only.

66. The Rock that is Higher.

E. JOHNSON. W. G. FISCHER, by per.

1 Oh, sometimes the shadows are deep,
And rough seems the path to the goal,
And sorrows, how often they sweep
Like tempests down over the soul. *Cho.*

2 Oh, sometimes how long seems the day,
And sometimes how heavy my feet;

But toiling in life's dusty way,
The Rock's blessed shadow, how sweet!
Cho.

3 Oh, near to the Rock let me keep,
Or blessings, or sorrows prevail;
Or climbing the mountain way steep,
Or walking the shadowy vale.
Cho.—Then quick, &c.

Sing to me of Heaven. 67

Mrs. M. S. B. DANA, 1850. Dr. Wm. MILLER, 1854.

1. O sing to me of heav'n, When I am call'd to die; Sing songs, sing songs, sing songs of ho-ly ec-sta-cy, To waft my soul on high; To waft my soul on high, Sing songs of ho-ly ec-sta-cy To waft my soul on high.

2 When cold and sluggish drops
Roll off my marble brow :
|| Break forth || in songs of joyfulness,
Let heaven begin below.

3 When the last moment comes,
Oh, watch my dying face ;
|| To catch the bright || seraphic gleam,
Which o'er my features plays.

4 Then to my raptured soul,
Let one sweet song be given,

|| Let music cheer || me last on earth,
And greet me first in heaven.

5 Then close my sightless eyes,
And lay me down to rest,
|| And fold || my pale and icy hands
Upon my lifeless breast.

6 Then, round my senseless clay,
Assemble those I love,
|| And sing of heaven, || delightful heaven,
My glorious home above.

✶ Small notes for 3d, 4th, and 6th verses.

68. Beautiful River.

Written 1864.
Words and Music by Rev. R. LOWRY, by per.

3 On the bosom of the river,
  Where the Saviour-king we own,
We shall meet, and sorrow never
  'Neath the glory of the throne.
                              Cho.

4 Ere we reach the shining river,
  Lay we every burden down ;
Grace our spirits will deliver,
  And provide a robe and crown.
                              Cho.

5 At the smiling of the river,
  Rippling with the Saviour's face,
Saints. whom death will never sever,
  Lift their songs of saving grace.
                              Cho.

6 Soon we'll reach the shining river,
  Soon our pilgrimage will cease ;
Soon our happy hearts will quiver
  With the melody of peace.
                              Cho.

The Prince of My Peace. 69

Words by Rev. W. F. CRAFTS.   Music by W. G. FISCHER, by per.

1. I stand all bewildered with won-der, And gaze on the o-cean of love; And o-ver its waves to my spir-it Comes peace, like a heaven-ly dove.
2. I struggled and wrestled to win it, The blessing that setteth me free; But when I had ceased from my struggles, His peace Jesus gave unto me.

REFRAIN. The cross now covers my sins; The past is under the blood; I'm trusting in Je-sus for all; My will is the will of my God.

3 He laid His hand on me and healed me,
 And bade me be every whit whole;
I touched but the hem of His garment,
 And glory came thrilling my soul.
   Refr.

4 The Prince of my peace is now passing.
 The light of His face is on me;
But listen, beloved, He speaketh:
 "My peace I will give unto thee."
   Refr.

70. The True Friend.

Words and Music by W. BENNETT, by per.

1. There is no friend like Jesus, So merciful and true:
His blood from sin doth free us, His love is ever new;
No earthly friend can give such aid, Nor from our foes deliver;
The trusting heart He ne'er betrayed, He bids us hope forever.

2.
O sinner, come to Jesus,
  Give now thy wand'rings o'er;
And never, never, never
  Resist His spirit more:
Put far away vile unbelief,
  From guilty passions sever;
And, though thou art of sinners chief,
  He'll give thee joy forever.

3.
Come weary, heavy laden,
  He will thy burden bear;
Cheer all thy lonely pathway,
  And all thy sorrows share:
He'll take thee at life's parting breath,
  When earthly friendships sever;
He'll make thee conqu'ror over death,
  And crown thee His forever.

Only Thee. 71

FANNY J. CROSBY. 1872.

W. H. DOANE.
From "Royal Diadem," by per.

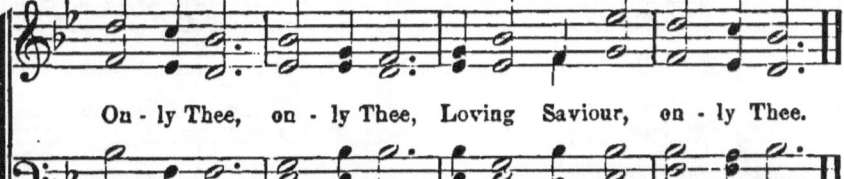

1. On - ly Thee, my soul's Redeemer! Whom have I in heaven beside?
Who on earth, with love so ten - der, All my wand'ring steps will guide?

CHORUS.
On - ly Thee, on - ly Thee, Loving Saviour, on - ly Thee.

2 Only Thee! no joy I covet
  But the joy to call thee mine—
Joy that gives the blest assurance,
  Thou hast owned and sealed me thine. *Cho.*

3 Only Thee! I ask no other;
  Thou art more than all to me;
Life, or health, or creature comfort,—
  I would give them all for thee. *Cho.*

4 Only Thee, whose blood has cleansed me,
  Would my raptured vision see,
While my faith is reaching upward,
  Ever upward, Lord to Thee. *Cho.*

72. Consecration.

Words by MARY D. JAMES.
Mrs. JOS. F. KNAPP, by per.
From "Notes of Joy."

1. My bod-y, soul and spir-it, Je-sus I give to Thee, A con-se-cra-ted off-'ring Thine ev-er more to be.
2. O Je-sus, might-y Sav-iour, I trust in Thy great name, I look for Thy sal-va-tion, Thy prom-ise now I claim.

CHORUS.
My all is on the Al-tar, I'm wait-ing for the fire,
ritard.
Waiting, wait-ing, wait-ing, I'm wait-ing for the fire.

3 O let the fire descending
  Just now upon my soul,
Consume my humble offering,
  And cleanse and make me whole.
      Cho.

4 I'm Thine, O blessed Jesus,
  Washed by Thy precious blood,
Now seal me by Thy Spirit
  A sacrifice to God. *Cho.*

The Blood! the precious Blood. 73

Words and Music by Rev. J. H. STOCKTON, by per.

1.
The cross! the cross! the blood-stained cross!
The hallow'd cross I see!
Reminding me of precious blood
That once was shed for me. *Cho.*

2.
The cross! the cross! the heavy cross,
The Saviour bore for me,
Which bowed him to the earth with grief,
On sad Mount Calvary. *Cho.*

3.
How light! how light! this precious cross,
Presented to my view;
And while, with care, I take it up,
Behold the crown my due. *Cho.*

4.
The crown! the crown! the glorious crown!
The crown of victory!
The crown of life! it shall be mine
When Jesus I shall see. *Cho.*

5.
My tears, unbidden, seem to flow
For love, unbounded love,
Which guides me through this world of woe,
And points to joys above. *Cho.*

74. Sweet Rest.

Rev. F. BOTTOME. D. D. SIR HENRY R. BISHOP.

Rest, rest, sweet, sweet rest, In the bosom of Je-sus there on-ly is rest.

1 O, ye that are weary and laden of soul,
Come, come to the fountain that maketh you whole.
There's peace in believing, there's rest in His name,
There's healing for all in the blood of the Lamb. *Cho.*

2 O cease from your anguish ye toilers for life,
For vain is your labor and fruitless your strife,
No hope can they bring you, no joy to your heart,
None, none but the Saviour can resting impart. *Cho.*

3 Then come to the Saviour ye weary and worn,
Your burdens and sorrows for you he hath borne.
No anguish that pierceth but pierced him before,
No thorn is so sharp as the crown which he wore. *Cho.*

4 Rest, rest blessed Jesus, O sweet rest at last,
Like calm on the ocean when tempest is past ;
The morning-light breaketh in joy from above,
And illumines my soul with His rainbow of love. *Cho.*

Sweet Hour of Prayer.   75

Words by Rev. W. W. WALFORD, 1849.   Wm. B. BRADBURY, by per.

2.
Sweet hour of prayer! sweet hour of pray-
Thy wings shall my petition bear,   [er!
To him whose truth and faithfulness,
Engage the waiting soul to bless;
And since he bids me seek his face,
Believe his word, and trust his grace,
‖: I'll cast on him my every care.
And wait for thee, sweet hour of prayer.:‖

3.
Sweet hour of prayer! sweet hour of pray-
May I thy consolation share;   [er!
Till, from Mount Pisgah's lofty height,
I view my home, and take my flight:
This robe of flesh I'll drop, and rise
To seize the everlasting prize;
‖: And shout, while passing thro' the air,
Farewell, farewell, sweet hour of prayer,:‖

76. Jesus, I my Cross have taken.

HENRY F. LYTE, 1825.   Air, Mozart. Arr. by H. P. M.

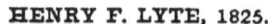

1. Jesus, I my cross have taken, All to leave and follow thee;
Naked, poor, despised, forsaken, Thou, from hence, my all shall be:
Perish every fond ambition, All I've sought, or hoped, or known;
Yet how rich is my condition! God and heaven are still my own.

2 Let the world despise and leave me,
  They have left my Saviour, too;
Human hearts and looks deceive me;
  Thou art not, like them, untrue:
And while thou shalt smile upon me,
  God of wisdom, love, and might,
Foes may hate, and friends may scorn me;
  Show thy face and all is bright.

3 Man may trouble and distress me,
  'T will but drive me to thy breast;
Life with trials hard may press me,
  Heaven will bring me sweeter rest.

Oh! 'tis not in grief to harm me
  While thy love is left to me,
Oh! 'twere not in joy to charm me,
  Were that joy unmixed with thee.

4 Soul, then know thy full salvation,
  Rise o'er sin, and fear, and care,
Joy to find in every station
  Something still to do or bear.
Soon shall close thy earthly mission,
  Soon shall pass thy pilgrim days;
Hope shall change to glad fruition,
  Faith to sight, and prayer to praise.

He leadeth Me. 77

2.
Sometimes 'mid scenes of deepest gloom,
Sometimes where Eden's bowers bloom,
By waters still, o'er troubled sea.—
Still 'tis his hand that leadeth me.
Refr.

3.
Lord, I would clasp thy hand in mine,
Nor ever murmur nor repine—
Content, whatever lot I see,
Since 'tis my God that leadeth me. *Refr.*

4.
And when my task on earth is done,
When, by thy grace, the victory's won,
E'en death's cold wave I will not flee,
Since God through Jordan leadeth me. *Refr.*

78   Near the Cross.

FANNY CROSBY. 1869.   From "Songs of Devotion," by per.   W. H. DOANE

1. Je-sus keep me near the cross, There a pre-cious Foun-tain,
Free to all a heal-ing stream, Flows from Calvary's mountain.

CHORUS.
In the Cross, In the Cross, Be my glo-ry ev-er;
Till my raptured soul shall find Rest be-yond the riv-er.

2 Near the Cross, a trembling soul,
   Love and mercy found me;
There the bright and morning star
   Shed its beams around me. *Cho.*

3 Near the Cross! oh, Lamb of God,
   Bring its scenes before me;
Help me walk from day to day
   With its shadow o'er me. *Cho.*

4 Near the Cross I'll watch and wait
   Hoping, trusting ever,
Till I reach the golden strand,
   Just beyond the river, *Cho.*

My Goal is Christ. 79

S. J. VAIL, by per.

1. Ah, tell me not of gold or treasure, Of pomp and beauty here on earth! There's not a thing that gives me pleasure Of all the world displays for worth. Each heart will seek and love its own; My goal is Christ, and Christ alone. My goal is Christ, and Christ alone.

2 The world and her pursuits will perish;
Her beauty's fading like a flower;
The brightest schemes the earth can cherish
Are but the pastime of an hour.
Each heart, etc.

3 Against this tower there's no prevailing;
His kingdom passes not away;
His throne abides, despite assailing,
From henceforth unto endless day.
Each heart, etc.

4 And tho' a pilgrim I must wander,
Still absent from the One I love,
He soon will have me with him yonder
In his own glory-realms above.
Triumphantly I therefore own,
||: My goal is Christ, and Christ alone. :||

Almost Persuaded. 81

Words and Music by P. P. BLISS, by per.

1. "Almost persuaded" now to believe; "Almost persuaded" Christ to receive. Seems now some soul to say, "Go, spirit, go thy way, Some more convenient day On thee I'll call."

2.
"Almost persuaded" come, come today;
"Almost persuaded," turn not away.
Jesus invites you here,
Angels are ling'ring near,
Prayers rise from hearts so dear;
  O wand'rer, come!

3.
"Almost persuaded," harvest is past;
"Almost persuaded" doom comes at last!
"Almost" cannot avail;
"Almost" is but to fail!
Sad, sad that bitter wail—
"Almost, *but lost!*"

3.
Tell me the story softly,
  With earnest tones, and grave;
Remember! I'm the sinner
  Whom Jesus came to save.
Tell me that story always,
  If you would really be,
In any time of trouble,
  A comforter to me.

4.
Tell me the same old story,
  When you have cause to fear
That this world's empty glory
  Is costing me too dear,
Yes, and when that world's glory
  Is drawing on my soul,
Tell me the old, old story:
  "Christ Jesus makes thee whole."

Tune on page 60.

82. I am Waiting by the River.

Wm. O. CUSHING.   Dr. Thos. HASTINGS.

1. I am wait-ing by the riv-er, And my heart has waited long;
Now I think I hear the cho-rus Of the an-gels welcome song,
Oh, I see the dawn is break-ing On the hill-tops of the blest,
"Where the wick-ed cease from troub-ling, And the wea-ry be at rest."

2.
Far away beyond the shadows
Of this weary vale of tears,
There the tide of bliss is sweeping
Through the bright and changeless years;
O! I long to be with Jesus,
In the mansions of the blest,
"Where the wicked cease from troubling,
And the weary be at rest."

3.
They are launching on the river,
From the calm and quiet shore,
And they soon will bear my spirit
Where the weary sigh no more;
For the tide is swiftly flowing,
And I long to greet the blest,
"Where the wicked cease from troubling,
And the weary be at rest."

3.
When His name was quite unknown,
  And sin my life employed;
Then He watched me as His own,
  Or I had been destroyed:
Now his mercy-seat I know,
  And now, by grace, am reconcil'd;
Would he spare me while a foe,
  To leave me when a child?

4.
If he shed his precious blood
  To bring me to his fold,
Can I think that meaner good
  He ever will withold?
Vain the tempter's dark device!
  For here my hope rests well assured,
In that great redemption price
  I see the whole secured.

"Gospel Magazine," May, 1775.

84. Nothing but Leaves.

W. S. C. S. J. VAIL, by per.

2 Nothing but leaves, no gathered sheaves,
   Of life's fair ripening grain;
   We sow our seeds, lo! tares and weeds,
   Words, *idle* words for earnest deeds,
   We reap with toil and pain,—
   ‖: Nothing but leaves!:‖

3 Nothing but leaves, sad memory weaves;
   No vail to hide the past,
   And as we trace our weary way,
   Counting each lost and misspent day
   Sadly we find at last—
   ‖: Nothing but leaves!:‖

4 Ah! who shall thus the Master meet,
   Bearing but withered leaves?
   Ah! who shall at the Saviour's feet,
   Before the awful judgment-seat
   Lay down, for golden sheaves
   ‖: Nothing but leaves!:‖

Tell me, Jesus. 35

Words by D. T. M.   Music by D. T. MACFARLAN.

1. Tell me, Je-sus, tell me now, While to thee I humbly bow,
Wilt thou take this heart of mine, And for-ev-er, seal it thine?
Wilt thou come and there a-bide, While I see thy o-pened side;
Pouring forth the streams of life, Giv-ing strength and end-ing strife!

2 If I yield myself to thee,
Wilt thou come direct to me,
And within thy loving arms
Cause my heart to feel thy charms?
Wilt thou, O my precious Lord,
Give me comfort by thy word,
By thy truth great joy impart
To my poor and throbbing heart?

3 Hark! I hear my Saviour say,
Come, my child, oh, come this way;
Take my hand, and walk with me
In the path I trod for thee;
Look by faith and see the blood
Sprinkled on the thorny road;
See, my child, each step I trod
Brings thee nearer to thy God.

4 Give thy heart, thyself to me,
Give whate'er I ask of thee;
Yield up all without restraint,
Free from murmur or complaint;
Then I'll take that heart of thine,
And with perfect love divine,
Make it new and pure within,
Spotless from all inbred sin.

86. I am coming, Lord!

Words by Rev. L. H.   Music by Rev. L. HARTSOUGH, by per.

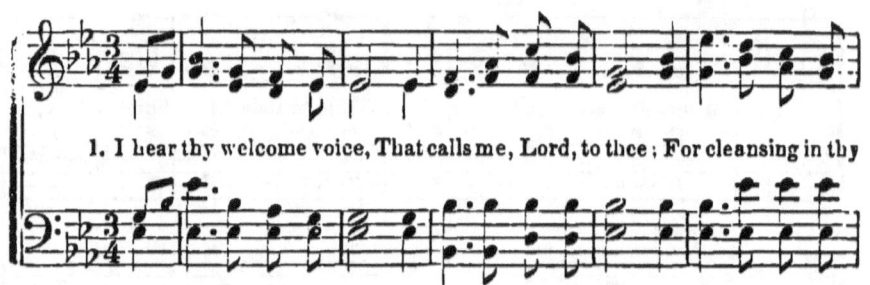

1. I hear thy welcome voice, That calls me, Lord, to thee; For cleansing in thy

precious blood, That flow'd on Calva-ry.   CHORUS.   I am coming, Lord!

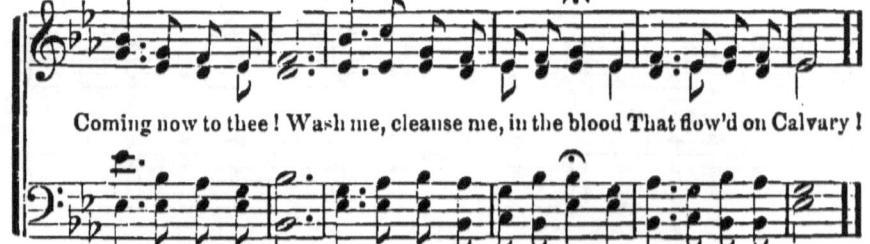

Coming now to thee! Wash me, cleanse me, in the blood That flow'd on Calvary!

2.
Though coming weak and vile,
 Thou dost my strength assure;
Thou dost my vileness fully cleanse,
 Till spotless all, and pure.

3.
'Tis Jesus calls me on
 To perfect faith and love,
To perfect hope, and peace, and trust,
 For earth and heaven above.

4.
And he the witness gives
 To loyal hearts and free,
That every promise is fulfilled,
 If faith but brings the plea.

5.
All hail! atoning blood!
 All hail! redeeming grace!
All hail! the gift of Christ, our Lord,
 Our strength and righteousness.

I'm Happy. 87

Arr by S. J. VAIL.

1. I'm happy, I'm happy, O wondrous account! My joys are immortal; I stand on the mount! I gaze on my treasure, And long to be there, With Jesus and angels, My kindred so dear.

2 O Jesus, my Saviour,
With thee I am blest!
My life and salvation,
My joy and my rest!
Thy name be my theme,
And thy love be my song,
Thy grace shall inspire
Both my heart and my tongue.

Look, look to Jesus!

Rev. E. P. HAMMOND. 1873.

HUBERT P. MAIN, by per.
From "Song Evangel."

1 Look, look to Jesus!
Behold a fountain free
Is open there for thee!
Look, look to Jesus!

2 Look, look to Jesus!
For thee he intercedes,—
His blood for thee now pleads,—
Look, look to Jesus!

3 Look, look to Jesus!
He's calling now for thee;
Poor sinner, look to me,—
Look, look to Jesus!

4 Look, look to Jesus!
If thou would'st live above
Where all is peace and love,
Look, look to Jesus!

88 There's a land far away.

*Words by JAS. G. CLARK. Arr. by H. P. MAIN

1. There's a land far a-way 'mid the stars we are told, Where they know not the sor-rws of time;
   Where the pure wa-ters flow, thro' the val-leys of gold, And where life is a trea-sure sublime:
   D.C. Where the way-wea-ry trav-el-er reach-es his goal, On the ev-er-green mountains of life.

'Tis the land of our God—'tis the home of the soul, Where the a-ges of splendor e-ter-nal-ly roll;

2 Here our gaze can not soar to that beautiful land,
   But our visions have told of its bliss ;
  And our souls by the gale from its gardens are fanned,
   When we faint in the deserts of this.
  And we sometimes have longed for its holy repose
   When our hearts have been rent with temptations and woes,
  And we've drank from the tide of the river that flows
   From the ever-green mountains of life.

3 Oh the stars never tread the blue heavens at night,
   But we think where the ransomed have trod ;
  And the day never smiles from his palace of light,
   But we feel the bright smile of our God.
  We are traveling home thro' earth's changes and gloom,
   To a region where pleasures unchangingly bloom,
  And our guide is the glory that shines thro' the tomb,
   From the ever-green mountains of life.

*Used by permission of O. Ditson & Co., owners of copyright.

Mary Magdalen.

I. B. WOODBURY, Arr.

3 She heard but the Saviour; she spoke but with sighs;
  She dare not look up to the heaven of his eyes:
  And the hot tears gush'd forth at each heave of her breast,
  As her lips to his sandals were throbbingly pressed.

4 In the sky, after tempest, as shineth the bow,
  In the glance of the sunbeam, as melteth the snow
  He looked on that lost one: "her sins were forgiven,"
  And Mary went forth in the beauty of heaven.

Believer. C. M.

Rev. J. NEWTON, 1779.   Arr. by HUBERT P. MAIN, 1855.

1. How sweet the name of Jesus sounds In a believer's ear; It soothes his sorrows, heals his wounds, And drives away his fear.

2 It makes the wounded spirit whole,
And calms the troubled breast;
T'is-manna to the hungry soul
And to the weary, rest.

3 Dear Name, the Rock on which I build,
My shield and hiding place;
My never-failing treasure filled
With boundless stores of grace.

4 Jesus, my Shepherd, Saviour, Friend,
My Prophet, Priest, and King,
My Lord, my Life, my Way, my End,
Accept the praise I bring.

5 I would thy boundless love proclaim
With every fleeting breath;
So shall the music of thy name
Refresh my soul in death.

Hamburg. L. M.

CHARLOTTE ELLIOTT, 1836.   Arr. by Dr. L. MASON.

1. Just as I am, with-out one plea, But that thy blood was shed for me, And that thou bidst me come to thee, O Lamb of God! I come. I come!

2 Just as I am, and waiting not
To rid my soul of one dark blot,
To thee, whose blood can cleanse each spot,
O Lamb of God! I come, I come!

3 Just as I am, though tossed about,
With many a conflict, many a doubt,
Fightings and fears within, without,
O Lamb of God! I come, I come!

4 Just as I am, poor, wretched, blind,
Sight, riches, healing of the mind,
Yea, all I need, in thee to find,
O Lamb of God! I come, I come!

5 Just as I am; thou wilt receive,
Wilt welcome, pardon, cleanse, relieve;
Because thy promise I believe,
O Lamb of God! I come, I come!

Jesus Loves Even Me. 91

Words and Music by P. P. BLISS, by per.

2 Though I forget him and wander away,
Kindly he follows wherever I stray;
Back to his dear loving arms would I flee,
When I remember that Jesus loves me. *Cho.*

3 Oh, if there's only one song I can sing,
When in his beauty I see the great King,
This shall my song in eternity be,
Oh, what a wonder that Jesus loves me. *Cho.*

92. Love of Jesus, all Divine.

Words by Dr. F. BOTTOME. Old Melody.

1. Love of Je-sus, all di-vine, Fill this longing heart of mine;
Ceaseless struggling aft-er life, Wea-ry with the end-less strife.
Sav-iour, Je-sus, lend thine aid, Lift thou up my fainting head!
Lead me to my long-sought rest, Pillowed on thy lov-ing breast.

2.
Thou alone my trust shall be,
Thou alone canst comfort me;
Only, Jesus, let thy grace
Be my shield and hiding-place;
Let me know thy saving power
In temptation's fiercest hour;
Then, my Saviour, at thy side
Let me evermore abide.

3.
Thou hast wrought this fond desire,
Kindled here this sacred fire,
Weaned my heart from all below,
Thee, and thee alone to know;
Thou who hast inspired the cry,
Thou alone canst satisfy;
Love of Jesus, all divine,
Fill this longing heart of mine.

And Can it Be?

Rev. CHAS. WESLEY. JER. INGALLS, 1805. Arr.

1. And can it be that I should gain An int'rest in the Saviour's blood? Died he for me, who caus'd his pain? For me, who him to death pursued? A-mazing love! how can it be that thou, my Lord shouldst die for me? A-mazing love! how can it be That thou, my Lord, shouldst die for me?

2.
'Tis myst'ry all, th' Immortal dies!
  Who can explore his strange design?
In vain the first-born seraph tries
  To sound the depths of love divine;
'Tis mercy all! let earth adore:
  Let angel minds inquire no more.

3.
He left his Father's throne above;
  (So free, so infinite his grace!)
Emptied himself of all but love,
  And bled for Adam's helpless race;
'Tis mercy all, immense and free,
  For O, my God, it found out me!

4.
Long my imprisoned spirit lay
  Fast bound in sin and nature's night;
Thine eyes diffus'd a quick'ning ray:
  I woke; the dungeon flamed with light;
My chain fell off, my heart was free—
  I rose, went forth and followed thee.

5.
No condemnation now I dread;
  Jesus, with all in him, is mine;
Alive in him, my living Head,
  And clothed in righteousness divine,
Bold I approach th' eternal throne
  And claim the crown thro' Christ my own.

94 Like the Sound of many Waters.

FANNY J. CROSBY, 1873.   HUBERT P. MAIN, by per.

1. Like the sound of many waters Rolling on, thro' a-ges long;
In a tide of rapture breaking,—Hark! the mighty cho-ral song!

CHORUS.
Hal-le-lu-jah! hal-le-lu-jah! Let the heavenly por-tals ring!
Christ is born, the Prince of glo-ry! Christ the Lord, Messiah, King!

2.
Lo! the Morning Star appeareth,
O'er the world His beams are cast;
He the Alpha and Omega,
He, the Great, the First the Last!
Hallelujah, etc.

3.
Clap your hands with exultation!
Sing aloud, rejoice with mirth,
Peace her silver wing hath folded:—
Lo! she comes to dwell on earth!
Hallelujah, etc.

4.
Saviour, not with costly treasure,
Do we gather at Thy throne.
All we have, our hearts we give Thee,—
Consecrate them Thine alone.
Hallelujah, etc.

Rest for the Weary. 95

Rev. J. Y. HARMER.   Rev. W. McDONALD, 1858, by per.

2.
He is fitting up my mansion,
  Which eternally shall stand ;
For my stay shall not be transient,
  In that holy, happy land.

3.
Pain nor sickness ne'er shall enter,
  Grief nor woe my lot shall share ;
But in that celestial center
  I a crown of life shall wear.

4.
Death itself shall then be vanquished,
  And his sting shall be withdrawn ;
Shout for gladness, oh ye ransomed,
  Hail with joy the rising morn,

5.
Sing, oh sing, ye heirs of glory !
  Shout your triumph as you go !
Zion's gate will open for you,
  You shall find an entrance through.

96. Carrie. 7s, 6s & 8s.

C. WESLEY, 1742.   HUBERT P. MAIN. by per.

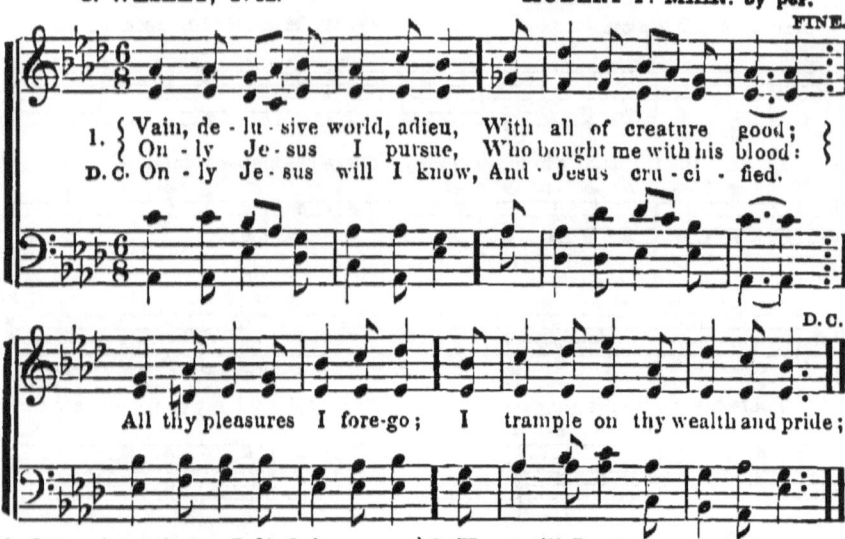

1. Vain, delusive world, adieu, With all of creature good;
Only Jesus I pursue, Who bought me with his blood:
D.C. Only Jesus will I know, And Jesus crucified.
All thy pleasures I forego; I trample on thy wealth and pride;

2 Other knowledge I disdain ;
'Tis all but vanity :
Christ the Lamb of God, was slain,—
He tasted death for me.
Me to save from endless woe,
The sin-atoning Victim died :
Only Jesus will I know,
And Jesus crucified:

3 Here will I set up my rest ;
My fluctuating heart
From the haven of his breast
Shall never more depart :
Whither should a sinner go?
His wounds for me stand open wide
Only Jesus will I know,
And Jesus crucified.

Penitence.

C. WESLEY, 1749.   W. H. OAKLEY.

1 Jesus, let thy pitying eye
Call back a wand'ring sheep ;
False to thee, like Peter, I
Would fain like Peter weep.
Let me be by grace restored ;
On me be all long suffering shown ;
Turn, and look upon me, Lord,
And break my heart of stone.

I Love Thee. 11s. 97

JER. INGALLS, 1805.   Arr. by HUBERT P. MAIN.

1. I love thee, I love thee, I love thee, my Lord; I love thee, my Saviour; I love thee, my God; I love thee, I love thee, and that thou dost know; But how much I love thee I nev-er can show.

  2 I'm happy, I'm happy, O wondrous account!
    My joys are immortal; I stand on the mount!
    I gaze on my treasure, and long to be there,
    With Jesus and angels, my kindred so dear.
  3 O Jesus, my Saviour, with thee I am blest!
    My life and salvation, my joy and my rest!
    Thy name be my theme, and thy love be my song,
    Thy grace shall inspire both my heart and my tongue.
  4 O, who's like my Saviour? He's Salem's bright King;
    He smiles, and He loves me, and helps me to sing;
    I'll praise him, I'll praise him with notes loud and shrill,
    While rivers of pleasure my spirit doth fill.

2.	3.
Saviour, Prince, enthroned above,	For thine own compassion's sake,
Repentance to impart,	The gracious wonder show;
Give me, through thy dying love,	Cast my sins behind thy back,
The humble, contrite heart:	And wash me white as snow;
Give what I have long implored,	If thy bowels now are stirr'd.
A portion of thy grief unknown;	If now I do myself bemoan,
Turn, and look upon me, Lord,	Turn, and look upon me, Lord,
And break my heart of stone.	And break my heart of stone.

Tune, PENITENCE, page 96.

98 I am waiting for the Saviour.

Rev. F. BOTTOME, D. D. 1873.   C. W. SANDERS.

1. I am wait-ing for the Saviour, And my heart has waited long;
Tell me, do I hear his footsteps, Is he com-ing with the throng?

CHORUS.
O thou son of David hear me, Take a - way this film of night;
With thy glorious presence cheer me, Speak, and let there now be light.

2 Long my troubled soul has waited
  Low in abject sorrow bowed;
Will he never hear my crying?
  Will he never lift the cloud? *Cho.*

3 All the world is filled with wonder
  At his mighty deeds of grace;
Devils at his presence tremble,
  Darkness flies before his face. *Cho.*

4 Art thou coming, O my Saviour?
  Do I hear thy sacred voice?

Shall my sightless eyes behold thee?
Shall my weeping soul rejoice? *Cho.*

5 Hark! He calls me! lo! the healing,
  Balm and blessing at his word!
Light thro' all my senses stealing,
  Lo! I look upon my Lord!
Cho.—O thou Son of David hear me,
  Let me never lose the sight,
Keep, O keep me ever near thee,
  Bathing in the hallowed light.

The Surrender.

C. WESLEY, 1749. WEISENTHAL.

1. How oft have I the Spirit griev'd, Since first with me he strove; How obstinately disbelieved, And trampled on his love! How have I sinn'd against the light: Broken from his embrace; And would not when I freely might Be justified by grace.

2 But after all that I have done
  To drive him from my heart,
The Spirit leaves me not alone,—
  He doth not yet depart;
He will not give the sinner o'er;
  Ready e'en now to save,
He bids me come as heretofore,
  That I his grace may have.

3 I take thee at thy gracious word;
  My foolishness I mourn;
And unto my redeeming Lord,
  However late, I turn.
Saviour. I yield, I yield at last;
  I hear thy speaking blood;
Myself, with all my sins, I cast
  On my atoning God.

(Tune, ZION.)

1 Guide me, O thou great Jehovah,
    Pilgrim through this barren land;
  I am weak, but thou art mighty,
    Hold me with thy powerful hand;
  Bread of heaven,
    Feed me till I want no more.

2 Open now the crystal fountain,
    Whence the healing streams do flow;
  Let the fiery, cloudy pillar,
    Lead me all my journey through;
  Strong Deliverer,
    Be thou still my strength and shield

3 When I tread the verge of Jordan,
    Bid my anxious fears subside;
  Bear me thro' the swelling current,
    Land me safe on Canaan's side;
  Songs of praises
    I will ever give to thee.

Wm. Williams. 1774.

100 The Solid Rock. L. M.

E. MOTE.   Wm. B. BRADBURY, by per.

1. My hope is built on nothing less Than Jesus' blood and righteousness;
I dare not trust the sweetest frame, But wholly lean on Jesus' name:
On Christ, the Solid Rock, I stand; All other ground is sinking sand, All other ground is sinking sand.

2.
When darkness seems to veil His face,
I rest on His unchanging grace ;
In every high and stormy gale,
My anchor holds within the vale :
  On Christ, the Solid Rock, I stand;
  All other ground is sinking sand.

3.
His oath, His covenant, and blood,
Support me in the whelming flood :
When all around my soul gives way,
He then is all my hope and stay :
  On Christ, the Solid Rock, I stand
  All other ground is sinking sand.

Full Salvation. 101

Words by LOUISE M. ROUSE. Music by Miss DORA BOOLE.

1. Precious Saviour, thou hast saved me: Thine, and only thine I am:
Oh! the cleansing blood has reached me, Glory, glo-ry to the Lamb!

CHORUS.
Glo-ry, glo-ry, Je-sus saves me, Glo-ry, glo-ry to the Lamb!
Oh! the cleansing blood has reached me, Glory, glo-ry to the Lamb.

2 Long my yearning heart was trying
To enjoy this perfect rest;
But I gave all trying over:
Simply trusting, I was blest.—*Cho.*

3 Trusting, trusting every moment;
Feeling now the blood applied;
Lying at the cleansing fountain;
Dwelling in my Saviour's side.—
Cho.

4 Consecrated to thy service,
I will live and die to thee:

I will witness to thy glory
Of salvation full and free,—*Cho.*

5 Yes, I will stand up for Jesus:
He has sweetly saved my soul,
Cleansed me from inbred corruption
Sanctified, and made me whole,—
Cho

6 Glory to the blood that bought me
Glory to its cleansing power!
Glory to the blood that keeps me!
Glory, glory, evermore!—*Cho.*

102. Jesus is Mine. 6s & 4s.

H. BONAR. THEO. E. PERKINS, by per.

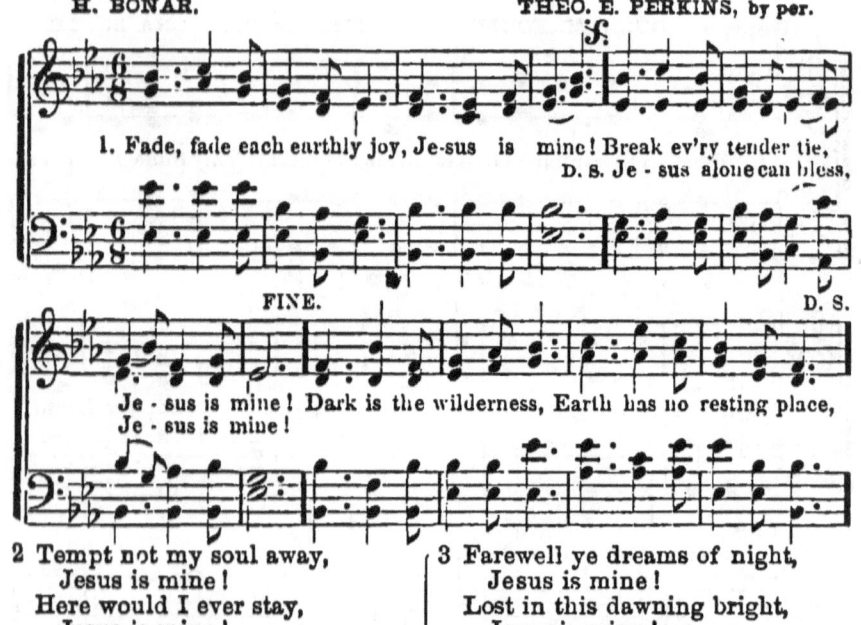

2 Tempt not my soul away,
　Jesus is mine!
　Here would I ever stay,
　Jesus is mine!
　Perishing things of clay,
　Born but for one brief day,
　Pass from my heart away,
　Jesus is mine!

3 Farewell ye dreams of night,
　Jesus is mine!
　Lost in this dawning bright,
　Jesus is mine!
　All that my soul has tried,
　Left but a dismal void,
　Jesus has satisfied,
　Jesus is mine!

Even Me. 8s, 7s & 3.

Mrs. E. CODNER, 1860. Wm. B. BRADBURY, by per.

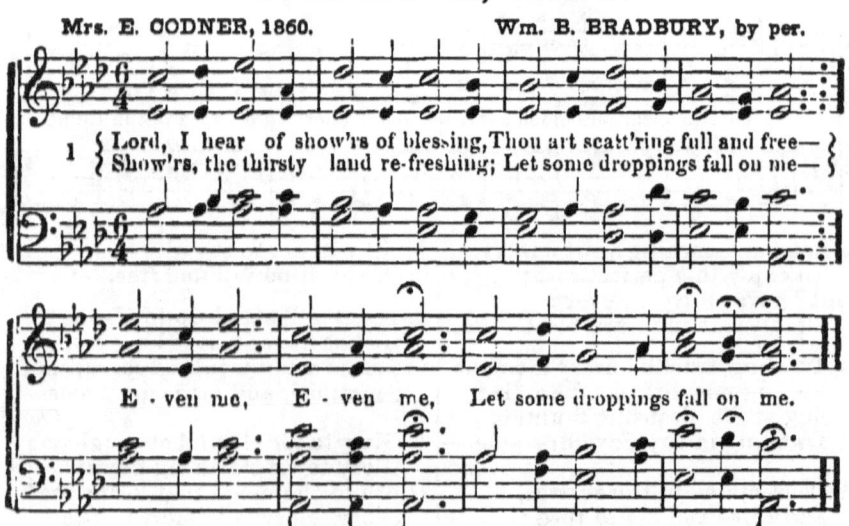

Bless me now.   103

ALEXANDER CLARK.
Pittsburgh, Pa.

ROBERT LOWRY.
From "Royal Diadem," by per.

1. Heavenly Father, bless me now; At the cross of Christ I bow;
Take my guilt and grief a-way; Hear and heal me now, I pray.

REFRAIN.
Bless me now, bless me now, Heavenly Fa-ther, bless me now.

2 Now, O Lord! this very hour,
Send thy grace and show thy power;
While I rest upon thy word,
Come and bless me now, O Lord!
Refr.
3 Now, just now, for Jesus' sake,
Lift the clouds, the fetters break;

While I look, and as I cry,
Touch and cleanse me ere I die.
Refr.
4 Never did I so adore
Jesus Christ, thy Son, before;
Now the time! and this the place!
Gracious Father, show thy grace.
Refr.

---

2 Pass me not, O God, my Father!
Sinful though my heart may be;
Thou might'st leave me, but the rather
Let thy mercy light on me—
Even me.

3 Pass me not, O gracious Saviour!
Let me live and cling to thee;
For I'm longing for thy favor;
Whilst thou'rt calling, oh! call me—
Even me.

4 Have I long in sin been sleeping
Long been slighting, grieving thee?
Has the world my heart been keeping?
Oh! forgive and rescue me—
Even me.

5 Pass me not, O mighty Spirit!
Thou canst make the blind to see;
Witnesser of Jesus' merit,
Speak some word of power to me—
Even me.

Tune, "EVEN ME," page 102.

104. Come nearer Jesus.

Words by FABER. Arr. by S J. VAIL.

1. There's a wide-ness in God's mer-cy, Like the wide-ness of the sea;
2. There's no place where earthly sorrows Are more felt than up in heaven,

There's a kind-ness in his jus-tice Which is more than lib - er - ty.
There's no place where earthly failings Have such kindly judgment given.

REFRAIN.

He is calling, "Come to me;" Lord, I'll glad-ly come to thee.

3 For the love of God is broader
 Than the measure of man's mind;
 And the heart of the Eternal
 Is most wonderfully kind. *Refr.*

4 But we make his love too narrow
 By false limits of our own;
 And we magnify his strictness
 With a zeal he will not own. *Refr.*

5 Pining souls! come nearer Jesus;
 Come, but come not doubting thus,
 Come with faith that trusts more freely
 His great tenderness for us. *Refr.*

6 If our love were but more simple
 We should take him at his word;
 And our lives would be all sunshine
 In the sweetness of our Lord. *Refr.*

GOD IS LOVE.

1 God is love; his mercy brightens
 All the path in which we rove;
 Bliss he wakes, and woe he lightens;
 God is wisdom, God is love. *Refr.*

2 Chance and change are busy ever;
 Man decays, and ages move;
 But his mercy waneth never;
 God is wisdom, God is love. *Refr.*

3 E'en the hour that darkest seemeth,
 Will his changeless goodness prove:
 From the gloom his brightness streameth,
 God is wisdom, God is love. *Refr.*

4 He with earthly cares entwineth
 Hope and comfort from above:
 Everywhere his glory shineth;
 God is wisdom, God is love. *Refr.*

J. Bowring.

Rathbun. 8s & 7s. 105

SIR JOHN BOWRING, 1825. ITHAMAR CONKEY.

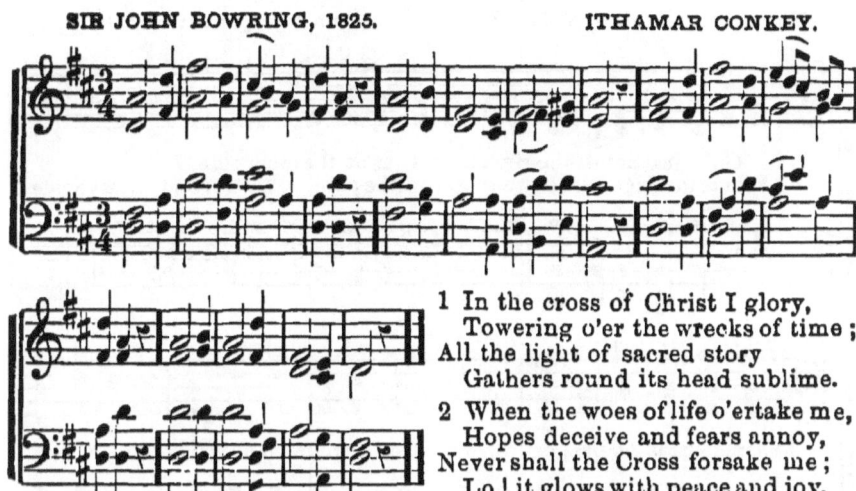

1 In the cross of Christ I glory,
 Towering o'er the wrecks of time ;
 All the light of sacred story
 Gathers round its head sublime.

2 When the woes of life o'ertake me,
 Hopes deceive and fears annoy,
 Never shall the Cross forsake me ;
 Lo ! it glows with peace and joy.

3 When the sun of bliss is beaming | From the Cross the radiance stream-
 Light and love upon my way, | Adds new lustre to the day. [ing,

Aletta. 7s.

LUCY LARCOM. Wm. B. BRADBURY, by per.

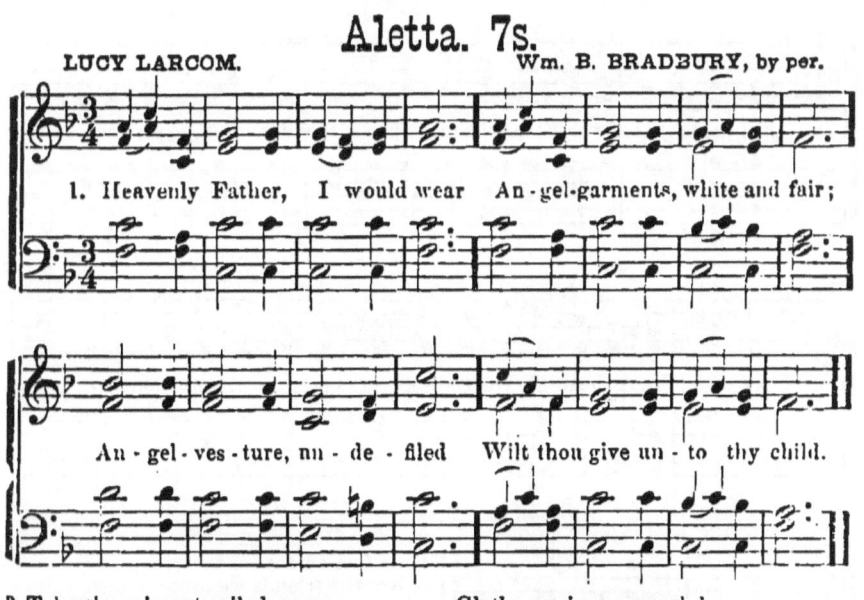

2 Take the raiment soiled away,
 That I wear with shame to-day:
 Give my angel robes to me,
 White with heaven's own purity.

3 Take away my cloak of pride,
 And the worthless rags 'twould hide ;

Clothe me in my angel dress.
 Beautiful with holiness.

4 Let me wear the white robes here,
 E'en on earth, my Father dear,
 Holding fast thy hand, and so,
 Through the world unspotted go.

106   Only just across the River!

Words by Mrs. M. A. KIDDER.   Wm. H. DOANE.
From "Bright Jewels," by per.

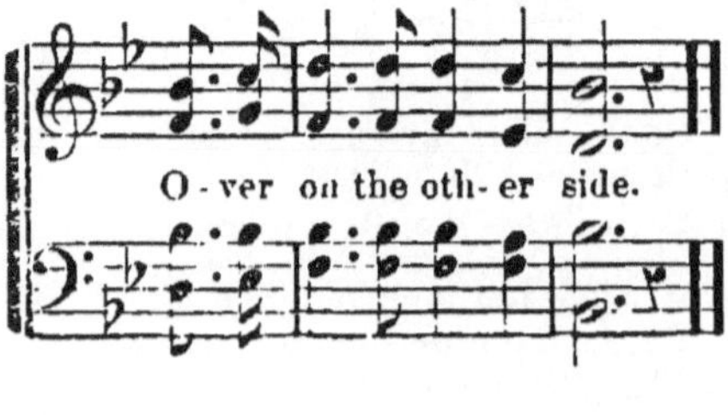

1. Only just across the river, Ov-er on the other side,
Where the angels are in waiting, And the pure .... in heart abide;
Where there is no pain or sorrow To intrude on heavenly rest, On-ly just across the riv-er, Stand the mansions of the blest.

CHORUS.

Only just across the river, Where the saints are passing over, On-ly just across the riv-er.

O-ver on the oth-er side.

2.
Only just across the river,
  Are the friends we loved below,
Clad in pure and spotless garments,
  That are whiter than the snow;
They have braved cold Jordan's billows,
  And have pass'd thro' death's alarms,
They are free from every sorrow,
  In the Saviour's loving arms. *Cho.*

Abide with Me! 107

FANNY J. CROSBY, 1865.   SYLVESTER MAIN, 1865.

1. Je-sus, Saviour, hear my call, Sin-ful though my heart may be,

Thou, my life, my hope, my all, Lord, a-bide with me.

2 Lonely in a stranger land,
Cast me not away from thee,
Lead me by thy gentle hand,
Lord, abide with me.

3 Thou hast died the lost to save,
Died to set the captive free,
Thou didst triumph o'er the grave,
Lord, abide with me.

4 Fill me with thy love divine,
Consecrate my life to thee,
Bend my stubborn will to thine,
Lord, abide with me.

5 When the shades of death prevail,
Father, let me cling to thee;
When I pass the gloomy vale,
Still abide with me.

6 Then, O then, my raptured soul
Heaven's eternal rest shall see;
There, while endless ages roll,
Live and reign with thee.

Tune, "ONLY JUST ACROSS THE RIVER." Page 106.

3 Only just across the river,
  Where the hills of glory shine,
There the pearly gates unfolding,
  Lead the soul to joy divine.
There the tree of life is blooming,
  And the living waters glide,
Only just across the river,
  Over on the other side. *Cho.*

4 Only just across the river
  Are the robes of spotless white;
Only just across the river
  Are the crowns of glory bright,
And the saints and angels joining
  In the songs with one accord,
Only just across the river,
  Sing the praises of the Lord. *Cho.*

108 Faber.

Rev. F. W. FABER.   Miss CARRIE Mc DONALD.

1. Dear Lord thy loving greatness ever lies, Outside us like a boundless sea,
2. Thus doth thy grandeur make us grand ourselves, 'Tis goodness always bids us fear;

We cannot lose ourselves where all is home Nor drift a-way from thee.
Thy greatness makes us brave as children are When those they love are near.

3.
Great God! our lowliness takes heart
  to play
Beneath the shadow of Thy state,
The only comfort of our littleness,
Is that Thou art so great.

4.
Then on Thy grandeur I will lay me
  down;
Already life is heaven for me;
No cradled child more softly lies than
I,—   Come soon eternity!

Thine, Lord, forever!

W. BENNETT, 1868.   HUBERT P. MAIN, by per.

1. Thine, Lord, forev - er, Purchased by blood di-vine, Rescued and
2. Thine, Lord, forev - er, Thro' storm and tempest wild, Trusting con-
3. Thine, Lord, forev - er, Cheered by thy precious word, Thro' darkness,

saved by thee, Lord, I am thine.
fi - ding-ly,   I am thy child.
doubts, and fears; Thine, thine, O Lord.

4.
Thine, Lord, forever,
  Tho' death shall lay me low,
  E'en in that dreadful hour,
Thine, Lord, I know.

5.
Thine, Lord, forever,
  When safe before thy throne
I stand, for evermore
Thine, thine, alone.

Beloved. 11s & 8s. 109

JOS. SWAIN, 1792. FREEMAN LEWIS, 1813. Arr.

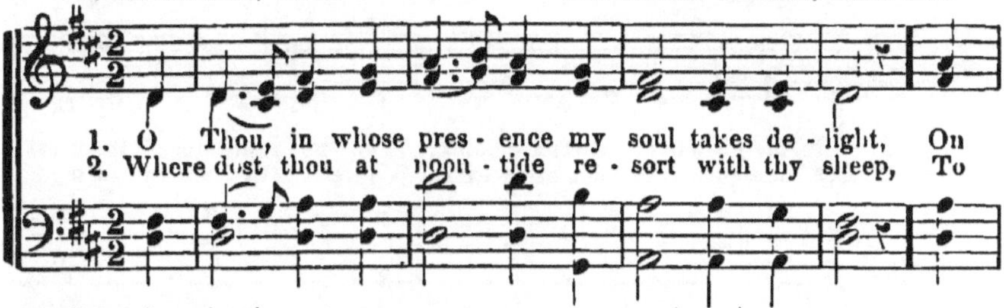

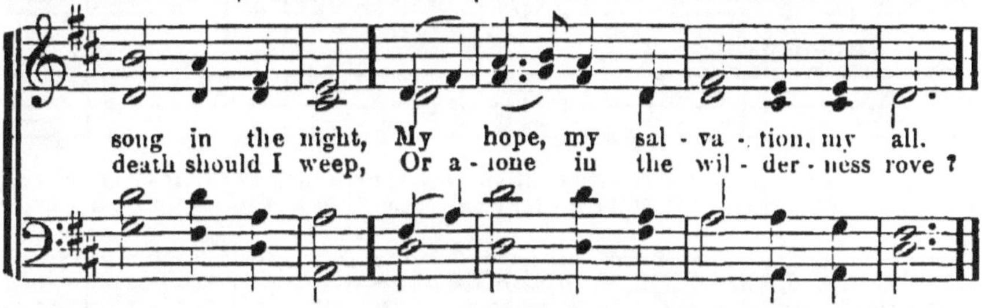

1. O Thou, in whose pres-ence my soul takes de-light,
On whom, in af-flic-tion I call;
My com-fort by day, and my song in the night,
My hope, my sal-va-tion, my all.

2. Where dost thou at noon-tide re-sort with thy sheep,
To feed in the pas-ture of love?
For why in the val-ley of death should I weep,
Or a-lone in the wil-der-ness rove?

3 O, why should I wander, an alien from thee,
Or cry in the desert for bread?
Thy foes will rejoice when my sorrows they see,
And smile at the tears I have shed.

4 He looks, and ten thousands of angels rejoice,
And myriads wait for his word;
He speaks, and eternity, fill'd with his voice,
Re-echoes the praise of the Lord.

Retreat. L. M.

1.
From every stormy wind that blows,
From every swelling tide of woes,
There is a calm, a sure retreat;
'T is found beneath the mercy-seat.

2.
There is a place where Jesus sheds
The oil of gladness on our heads—
A place than all besides, more sweet,
It is the blood-bought mercy-seat.

3.
There is a scene where spirits blend,
Where friend holds fellowship with friend;
Tho' sundered far, by faith they meet
Around one common mercy-seat.

4.
There, there, on eagle wings we soar,
And sin and sense molest no more;
And heaven comes down our souls to greet,
And glory crowns the mercy-seat.

HUGH STOWELL. 1828.

110. Let Me Go!

Words by Rev. L. H.
Rev. L. HARTSOUGH, by per.

3 Let me go, why should I tarry?
  What has earth to bind me here?
 What, but cares and toils and sorrows?
  What, but death and pain and fear!
 Let me go, for hopes most cherish'd
  Blasted round me often lie,
 O! I've gathered brightest flowers
  But to see them fade and die.

4 Let me go where tears and sighing
  Are forever more unknown,
 Where the joyous songs of glory
  Call me to a happier home.
 Let me go—I'd cease this dying,
  I would gain life's fairer plains,
 Let me join the myriad harpers,
  Let me chant their rapturous strain.

I know Thou art gone! 111

Mrs MARY S. B. DANA. Wm. B. BRADBURY, by per.

1. I know thou art gone to the home of thy rest, Then why should my soul be so sad;
I know thou art gone where the weary are blest, And the mourner looks up and is glad.

CHORUS.
I nev-er look up with a wish to the sky, But a light like thy beauty is there;
And I hear a low murmur like thine in reply, When I pour out my spirit in prayer.

2. In thy far away home, wheresoe'er it may be,
I know thou hast visions of mine;
And my heart hath revealings of thine and of thee,
In many a token and sigh.
  I never look up, etc.

3. In the hush of the night, on the waste of the sea,
Or alone with the breeze on the hill;
I have ever a presence that whispers of thee,
And my spirit lies down and is still.
  I never look up, etc.

112   Harp. C. M.

S. WESLEY.   A. CHAPIN.

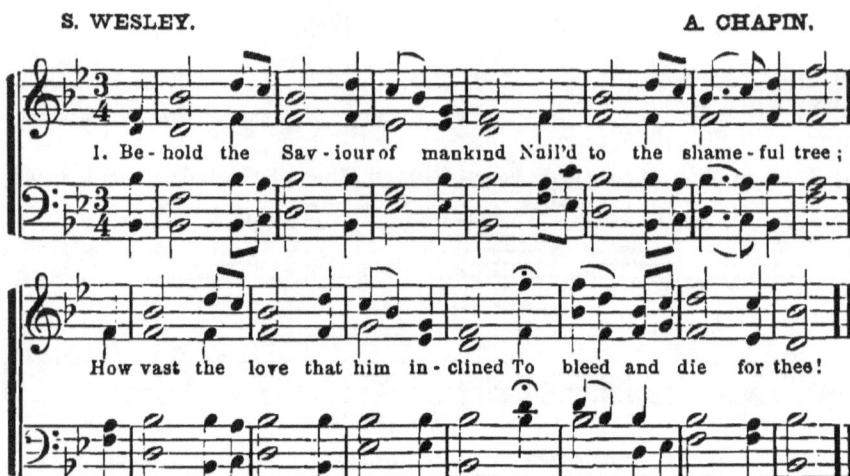

1. Be-hold the Sav-iour of mankind Nail'd to the shame-ful tree;
How vast the love that him in-clined To bleed and die for thee!

2 Hark, how he groans, while nature shakes,
And earth's strong pillars bend:
The temple's vail in sunder breaks,—
The solid marbles rend.
3 'Tis done! the precious ransom's paid!
Receive my soul! He cries;

See where he bows his sacred head;
He bows his head and dies.
4 But soon he'll break death's envious chain,
And in full glory shine:
O Lamb of God, was ever pain,
Was ever love, like thine?

Cross and Crown. C. M.

G. N. ALLEN.   A. CHAPIN.

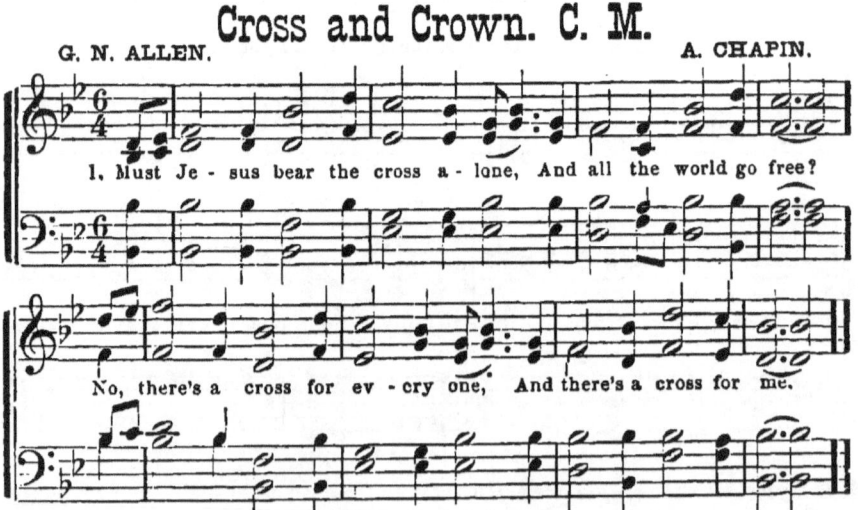

1. Must Je-sus bear the cross a-lone, And all the world go free?
No, there's a cross for ev-ery one, And there's a cross for me.

2 How happy are the saints above,
Who once went sorrowing here;
But now they taste unmingled love,
And joy without a tear.

3 The consecrated cross I'll bear,
Till death shall set me free;
And then go home my crown to wear,
For there's a crown for me!

Rest. L. M. 113

MARGARET MACKAY, 1832.   Wm. B. BRADBURY, by per.

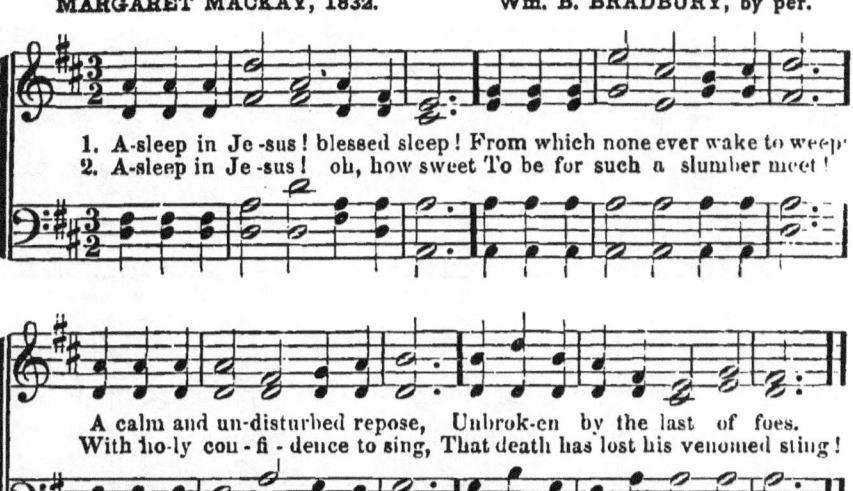

1. A-sleep in Je-sus! blessed sleep! From which none ever wake to weep
2. A-sleep in Je-sus! oh, how sweet To be for such a slumber meet!
A calm and un-disturbed repose, Unbrok-en by the last of foes.
With ho-ly cou-fi-dence to sing, That death has lost his venomed sting!

3 Asleep in Jesus! peaceful rest!
Whose waking is supremely blest;
No fear, no woe, shall dim that hour,
That manifests the Saviour's power,

4 Asleep in Jesus! oh, for me
May such a blissful refuge be!
Securely shall my ashes lie,
And wait the summons from on high,

Remember Me.

ASA HULL, by per.

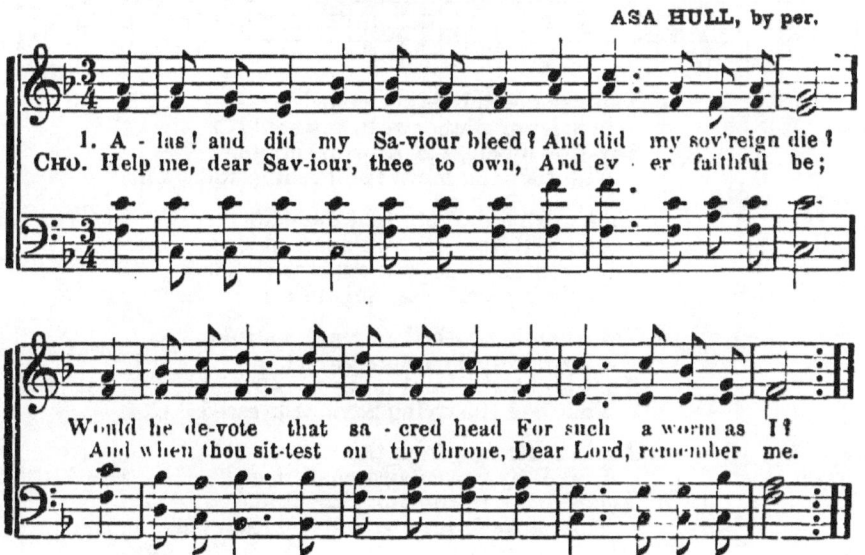

1. A-las! and did my Sa-viour bleed? And did my sov'reign die?
CHO. Help me, dear Sav-iour, thee to own, And ev-er faithful be;
Would he de-vote that sa-cred head For such a worm as I?
And when thou sit-test on thy throne, Dear Lord, remember me.

Peacefully Rest.

WILLIAM BATCHELDER BRADBURY.
From "Golden Chain," by per.

1. An-oth-er fleeting day is gone; Slow o'er the west the shadows rise; Swift the soft-stealing hours have flown, And night's dark mantle vails the skies.

CHORUS.
Peacefully rest, Peacefully rest, Rest till the morning, Peacefully rest.

2 Another fleeting day is gone;
   In solemn silence rest, my soul!
Bow down before His awful throne,
   Who bids the morn and evening roll. *Cho.*

3 Soon shall a darker night descend,
   And vail from me yon azure skies;
And soon shall death's oppressive hand
   Lie heavy on these languid eyes. *Cho.*

4 Yet when beneath the dreadful shade,
   I lay my weary frame to rest,
That night shall not make me afraid;
   That bed the dying Saviour pressed. *Cho.*

5 Again emerging from the night,
   I, like my risen Lord shall rise;
Again drink in the morning light,
   Pure at its fount above the skies. *Cho.*

The Dear Ones all at Home. 115

Rev. H. BONAR.
Wm. B. BRADBURY, by per.
From "Golden Shower."

3 Beyond the parting and the meeting,
   I shall be soon:
Beyond the farewell and the greeting,
Beyond the pulse's fever-beating;
   I shall be soon.
Love, rest, and home!
   Sweet, sweet home!
‖: O how sweet it will be there to meet
   The dear ones all at home. :‖

4 Beyond the frost-chain and the fever,
   I shall be soon:
Beyond the rock-waste and the river,
Beyond the ever and the never,
   I shall be soon.
Love, rest, and home!
   Sweet, sweet home!
‖: O how sweet it will be there to meet
   The dear ones all at home. :‖

Duane Street. L. M. 117

JOHN CENNICK, 1743. Rev. GEO. COLES.

2 This is the way I long have sought,
And mourn'd because I found it not;
My grief a burden long has been,
Because I was not saved from sin.
The more I strove against its power,
I felt its weight and guilt the more;
Till late I heard my Saviour say,—
Come hither, soul, I am the way.

3 Lo! glad I come; and thou blest Lamb,
Shalt take me to thee, as I am:
Nothing but sin have I to give,—
Nothing but love shall I receive.
Then will I tell to sinners round,
What a dear Saviour I have found;
I'll point to thy redeeming blood,
And say,—Behold the way to God.

118   If I were a Voice.

From "Song Crown," by per.   ISAAC BEVERLY WOODBURY.

If I were a Voice. 119

3 If I were a voice, a convincing voice,
  I'd travel with the wind,
And wherever I saw the nations torn,
By warfare, jealousy, spite or scorn,
  Or hatred of their kind,
I would fly, I would fly on the thunder crash,
And into their blinded bosoms flash;
Then, with their evil thoughts subdued,
I'd teach them Christian brotherhood,
  I would fly, I would fly,
I would fly on the thunder crash.

4 If I were a voice, an immortal voice,
  I would fly the earth around:
And wherever man to his idols bowed,
I'd publish in notes both long and loud
  The Gospel's joyful sound.
I would fly, I would fly on the wings of day,
Proclaiming peace on my world-wide way,
Bidding the saddened earth rejoice—
If I were a voice, an immortal voice,
  I would fly, I would fly,
I would fly on the wings of day.

Pilesgrove. L. M.

1 O thou, to whose all-searching sight
The darkness shineth as the light,
Search, prove my heart, it pants for thee;
O burst these bonds, and set it free.

2 Wash out its stains, refine its dross;
Nail my affections to the cross;
Hallow each thought; let all within
Be clean, as thou, my Lord, art clean.

3 If in this darksome wild I stray,
Be thou my light, be thou my way;
No foes, no violence I fear,
No fraud, while thou, my God, art near.

4 When rising floods my soul o'erflow,
When sinks my heart in waves of woe,
Jesus, thy timely aid impart,
And raise my head, and cheer my heart.

Windham. L. M.

1 Show pity, Lord, O Lord, forgive;
Let a repenting rebel live.
Are not thy mercies large and free?
May not a sinner trust in thee?

2 My crimes are great, but don't surpass
The power and glory of thy grace;
Great God, thy nature hath no bound—
So let thy pard'ning love be found.

3 O wash my soul from every sin,
And make my guilty conscience clean;
Here on my heart the burden lies,
And past offences pain my eyes.

4 My lips with shame my sins confess,
Against thy law, against thy grace;
Lord, should thy judgments grow severe,
I am condemn'd, but thou art clear.

Uxbridge. L. M.

1 Lord, I am thine, entirely thine,
Purchased and saved by blood divine;
With full consent thine I would be,
And own thy sov'reign right in me.

2 Grant one poor sinner more a place
Among the children of thy grace;
A wretched sinner, lost to God,
But ransom'd by Immanuel's blood.

3 Thine would I live, thine would I die;
Be thine through all eternity;
The vow is past beyond repeal,
And now I set the solemn seal.

4 Here, at that cross where flows the blood
That bought my guilty soul for God,
Thee, my new Master, now I call,
And consecrate to thee my all.

Forrest. L. M.

1 O that my load of sin were gone;
O that I could at last submit
At Jesus' feet to lay it down—
To lay my soul at Jesus' feet.

2 Rest for my soul I long to find:
Saviour of all, if mine thou art,
Give me thy meek and lowly mind,
And stamp thine image on my heart.

3 Break off the yoke of inbred sin,
And fully set my spirit free;
I cannot rest till pure within—
Till I am wholly lost in thee.

4 Fain would I learn of thee, my God;
Thy light and easy burden prove;
The cross all stain'd with hallow'd blood,
The labor of thy dying love.

Missionary Chant. L. M.

1 Ye Christian heralds, go proclaim
Salvation in Immanuel's name;
To distant climes the tidings bear,
And plant the rose of Sharon there.

2 He'll shield you with a wall of fire,
With holy zeal your hearts inspire,
Bid raging winds their fury cease,
And calm the savage breast to peace.

3 And when our labors all are o'er,
Then shall we meet to part no more—
Meet with the blood-bought throng to fall,
And crown the Saviour Lord of all.

Sessions. L. M.

1 I thirst, thou wounded Lamb of God,
To wash me in thy cleansing blood;
To dwell within thy wounds; then pain
Is sweet, and life or death is gain.

Winnowed Hymns. 121

2 Take my poor heart, and let it be
Forever closed to all but thee:
Seal thou my breast, and let no wear
That pledge of love forever there.

3 How blest are they who still abide
Close shelter'd in thy bleeding side!
Who thence their life and strength derive,
And by thee move, and in thee live.

4 What are our works but sin and death,
Till thou thy quick'ning Spirit breathe?
Thou giv'st the power thy grace to move;
O wondrous grace! O boundless love!

Northfield. C. M.

1 O for a thousand tongues, to sing
My great Redeemer's praise;
The glories of my God and King,
The triumphs of his grace.

2 My gracious Master, and my God,
Assist me to proclaim—
To spread, through all the earth abroad,
The honors of thy name.

3 Jesus!—the Name that charms our fears,
That bids our sorrows cease;
'Tis music in the sinner's ears,
'Tis life, and health, and peace.

4 He breaks the power of cancel'd sin,
He sets the pris'ner free;
His blood can make the foulest clean;
His blood avail'd for me.

Coronation. C. M.

1 All hail the power of Jesus' name!
Let angels prostrate fall;
Bring forth the royal diadem,
And crown him Lord of all.

2 Ye chosen seed of Israel's race,
Ye ransom'd from the fall,
Hail him who saves by his grace,
And crown him Lord of all.

3 Sinners, whose love can ne'er forget
The wormwood and the gall,
Go, spread your trophies at his feet,
And crown him Lord of all.

4 Let every kindred, every tribe,
On this terrestrial ball,
To him all majesty ascribe,
And crown him Lord of all.

Azmon. C. M.

1 O for a closer walk with God—
A calm and heavenly frame;
A light to shine upon the road
That leads me to the Lamb.

2 Where is the blessedness I knew
When first I saw the Lord?
Where is the soul-refreshing view
Of Jesus and his word?

3 What peaceful hours I once enjoy'd!
How sweet their mem'ry still!
But they have left an aching void
The world can never fill.

4 Return, O holy Dove, return,
Sweet messenger of rest:
I hate the sins that made thee mourn,
And drove thee from my breast.

Stephens. C. M.

1 O for a heart to praise my God,
A heart from sin set free;
A heart that always feels thy blood,
So freely spilt for me;

2 A heart resign'd, submissive, meek,
My great Redeemer's throne;
Where only Christ is heard to speak—
Where Jesus reigns alone.

3 O for a lowly, contrite heart,
Believing, true, and clean;
Which neither life nor death can part
From Him that dwells within;

4 A heart in every thought renew'd,
And full of love divine;
Perfect, and right, and pure, and good,
A copy, Lord, of thine.

Evan. C. M.

1 In mercy, Lord, remember me,
Through all the hours of night,
And grant to me most graciously
The safeguard of thy might.

2 With cheerful heart I close mine eyes,
Since thou wilt not remove;
O, in the morning let me rise
Rejoicing in thy love

3 Or, if this night should prove my last,
  And end my transient days;
  Lord, take me to thy promised rest,
  Where I may sing thy praise.

Avon. C. M.

1 Jesus, thine all-victorious love
  Shed in my heart abroad:
  Then shall my feet no longer rove,
  Rooted and fix'd in God.

2 O that in me the sacred fire
  Might now begin to glow;
  Burn up the dross of base desire,
  And make the mountains flow.

3 O that it now from heaven might fall,
  And all my sins consume:
  Come, Holy Ghost, for thee I call;
  Spirit of burning, come.

4 Refining fire, go through my heart;
  Illuminate my soul;
  Scatter thy life through every part,
  And sanctify the whole.

Ortonville. C. M.

1 Once more, my soul, the rising day
  Salutes thy waking eyes;
  Once more, my voice, thy tribute pay
  To Him that rules the skies.

2 Night unto night his name repeats,
  The day renews the sound;
  Wide as the heavens on which he sits,
  To turn the seasons round.

3 'Tis he supports my mortal frame;
  My tongue shall speak his praise;
  My sins might rouse his wrath to flame,
  But yet his wrath delays.

4 O God, let all my hours be thine,
  Whilst I enjoy the light;
  Then shall my sun in smiles decline,
  And bring a peaceful night.

Heber. C. M.

1 Come, humble sinner, in whose breast
  A thousand thoughts resolve,
  Come, with your guilt and fear oppress'd,
  And make this last resolve:

2 I'll go to Jesus, though my sin
  Like mountains round me close;
  I know his courts, I'll enter in,
  Whatever may oppose.

3 Prostrate I'll lie before his throne,
  And there my guilt confess;
  I'll tell him, I'm a wretch undone
  Without his sov'reign grace.

4 Perhaps he will admit my plea,
  Perhaps will hear my prayer;
  But, if I perish, I will pray,
  And perish only there.

5 I can but perish if I go—
  I am resolved to try;
  For if I stay away, I know
  I must forever die.

Varina. C. M. D.

1 There is a land of pure delight,
  Where saints immortal reign;
  Infinite day excludes the night,
  And pleasures banish pain.
  There everlasting spring abides,
  And never-with'ring flowers:
  Death, like a narrow sea, divides
  This heavenly land from ours.

2 Sweet fields beyond the swelling flood
  Stand dress'd in living green;
  So the Jews old Canaan stood,
  While Jordan roll'd between.
  Could we but climb where Moses stood,
  And view the landscape o'er.
  Not Jordan's stream, nor death's cold flood,
  Should fright us from the shore.

Gerar. S. M.

1 Give to the winds thy fears;
  Hope, and be undismay'd;
  God hears thy sighs and counts thy tears;
  God shall lift up thy head.

2 Through waves, and clouds, and storms,
  He gently clears thy way;
  Wait thou his time, so shall this night
  Soon end in joyous day.

3 Still heavy is thy heart?
  Still sink thy spirits down?
  Cast off the weight—let fear depart,
  And every care be gone.

4 What though thou rulest not;
  Yet heaven, and earth, and hell,
  Proclaim: God sitteth on the throne,
  And ruleth all things well.

Winnowed Hymns. 123

Kentucky. S. M.

1 A charge to keep I have,
  A God to glorify;
  A never-dying soul to save,
  And fit it for the sky.

2 To serve the present age,
  My calling to fulfill—
  O may it all my powers engage,
  To do my Master's will.

3 Arm me with jealous care,
  As in thy sight to live;
  And O, thy servant, Lord, prepare,
  A strict account to give.

4 Help me to watch and pray,
  And on thyself rely,
  Assured, if I my trust betray,
  I shall forever die.

Shirland. S. M.

1 Come, ye that love the Lord,
  And let your joys be known;
  Join in a song with sweet accord
  While ye surround his throne.

2 Let those refuse to sing
  Who never knew our God;
  But servants of the heavenly King
  May speak their joys abroad.

3 The God that rules on high,
  That all the earth surveys,
  That rides upon the stormy sky,
  And calms the roaring seas;

4 This awful God is ours,
  Our Father and our Love;
  He will send down his heavenly powers
  To carry us above.

Boylston. S. M.

1 And can I yet delay
  My little all to give?
  To tear my soul from earth away
  For Jesus to receive?

2 Nay, but I yield, I yield;
  I can hold out no more:
  I sink, by dying love compell'd,
  And own thee conqueror.

3 Though late, I all forsake;
  My friends, my all, resign:
  Gracious Redeemer, take, O take,
  And seal me ever thine.

4 Come, and possess me whole,
  Nor hence again remove;
  Settle and fix my wav'ring soul
  With all thy weight of love.

State Street. S. M.

1 My God, my life, my love,
  To thee, to thee I call:
  I cannot live, if thou remove,
  For thou art all in all.

2 Thy shining grace can cheer
  This dungeon where I dwell:
  'Tis paradise when thou art here,
  If thou depart, 'tis hell.

3 The smilings of thy face,
  How amiable they are!
  'Tis heaven to rest in thine embrace,
  And nowhere else but there.

4 To thee, and thee alone,
  The angels owe their bliss;
  They sit around thy gracious throne,
  And dwell where Jesus is.

Thatcher. S. M.

1 Thou very-present aid
  In suff'ring and distress;
  The mind which still on thee is stay'd
  Is kept in perfect peace.

2 The soul by faith reclined
  On the Redeemer's breast,
  'Mid raging storms, exults to find
  An everlasting rest.

3 Sorrow and fear are gone,
  Whene'er thy face appears;
  It stills the sighing orphan's moan,
  And dries the widow's tears.

4 It hallows every cross;
  It sweetly comforts me;
  Makes me forget my every loss,
  And find my all in thee.

Supplication. L. M. 6 lines.

1 Thou hidden Source of calm repose,
Thou all-sufficient Love divine,
My help and refuge from my foes,
Secure I am while thou art mine:
And lo! from sin, and grief, and shame,
I hide me, Jesus, in thy name.

2 Thy mighty name salvation is,
And keeps my happy soul above:
Comfort it brings, and power, and peace,
And joy, and everlasting love:
To me, with thy great name, are given
Pardon, and holiness, and heaven.

Carmarthen. H. M.

1 Let earth and heaven agree,
Angels and men be join'd,
To celebrate with me
The Saviour of mankind:
T' adore the all-atoning Lamb,
And bless the sound of Jesus' name.

2 Jesus! transporting sound!
The joy of earth and heaven;
No other help is found,
No other name is given,
By which we can salvation have;
But Jesus came the world to save.

3 Jesus! harmonious name!
It charms the host above;
They evermore proclaim,
And wonder at, his love:
'Tis all their happiness to gaze—
'Tis heaven to see our Jesus' face.

Pleyel's Hymn. 7s.

1 Depth of mercy! can there be
Mercy still reserved for me?
Can my God his wrath forbear?
Me, the chief of sinners, spare?

2 I have long withstood his grace;
Long provoked him to his face;
Would not hearken to his calls;
Grieved him by a thousand falls.

3 Now incline me to repent;
Let me now my sins lament;
Now my foul revolt deplore,
Weep, believe, and sin no more.

4 Kindled his relentings are;
Me he now delights to spare;
Cries, How shall I give thee up?—
Lets the lifted thunder drop.

Prayer. 7s.

1 Prince of peace, control my will;
Bid this struggling heart be still;
Bid my fears and doubtings cease—
Hush my spirit into peace.

2 Thou hast bought me with thy blood,
Open'd wide the gate to God:
Peace I ask—but peace must be,
Lord, in being one with thee.

3 May thy will, not mine, be done;
May thy will and mine be one:
Chase these doubtings from my heart;
Now thy perfect peace impart.

4 Saviour! at thy feet I fall;
Thou my life, my God, my all!
Let thy happy servant be
One for evermore with thee!

Toplady. 7s, 6 lines.

1 Rock of ages, cleft for me,
Let me hide myself in thee;
Let the water and the blood,
From thy wounded side which flow'd,
Be of sin the double cure—
Save from wrath and make me pure.

2 Could my tears forever flow,
Could my zeal no languor know,
These for sin could not atone;
Thou must save, and thou alone:
In my hand no price I bring;
Simply to the cross I cling.

3 While I draw this fleeting breath,
When my eyes shall close in death,
When I rise to worlds unknown,
And behold thee on thy throne,
Rock of ages, cleft for me,
Let me hide myself in thee.

Oron. 7s, 6 lines.

1 By thy birth, and by thy tears;
By thy human griefs and fears;
By thy conflict in the hour
Of the subtle tempter's power—
Saviour, look with pitying eye;
Saviour, help me, or I die.

Winnowed Hymns. 125

2 By the tenderness that wept
    O'er the grave where Laz'rus slept;
By the bitter tears that flow'd
    Over Salem's lost abode—
Saviour, look with pitying eye;
Saviour, help me, or I die.

3 By thy lonely hour of prayer;
    By the fearful conflict there;
By thy cross and dying cries;
By thy one great sacrifice—
Saviour, look with pitying eye;
Saviour, help me, or I die.

Martyn. 7s, double.

1 Jesus, lover of my soul,
    Let me to thy bosom fly,
While the nearer waters roll,
    While the tempest still is high;
Hide me, O my Saviour, hide,
    Till the storm of life is past;
Safe into the haven guide,
    O receive my soul at last.

2 Other refuge have I none;
    Hangs my helpless soul on thee:
Leave, O leave me not alone;
    Still support and comfort me:
All my trust on thee is stay'd;
    All my help from thee I bring;
Cover my defenceless head
    With the shadow of thy wing.

Bethany. 6s & 4s.

1 Nearer, my God, to thee,
    Nearer to thee!
E'en though it be a cross
    That raiseth me.
Still all my song shall be,
Nearer, my God, to thee,
    Nearer to thee!

2 Though like a wanderer,
    The sun gone down,
Darkness comes over me,
    My rest a stone;
Yet in my dreams I'd be
Nearer, my God, to thee,
    Nearer to thee!

3 There let my way appear
    Steps unto heaven;
All that thou sendest me
    In mercy given;
Angels to beckon me
Nearer, my God, to thee,
    Nearer to thee!

4 Or, if on joyful wing,
    Cleaving the sky,
Sun, moon, and stars forgot,
    Upward I fly,
Still all my song shall be,
Nearer, my God, to thee,
    Nearer to thee!

New Haven. 6s & 4s.

1 My faith looks up to thee,
    Thou Lamb of Calvary:
        Saviour divine,
Now hear me while I pray,
Take all my guilt away;
O let me, from this day,
    Be wholly thine.

2 May thy rich grace impart
Strength to my fainting heart;
    My zeal inspire;
As thou hast died for me,
O may my love to thee
Pure, warm, and changeless be—
    A living fire.

* The Convert. 12s & 9s.

1 O how happy are they
    Who the Saviour obey,
And have laid up their treasures above;
    Tongue can never express
    The sweet comfort and peace
Of a soul in its earliest love.

2 That sweet comfort was mine,
    When the favor divine
I received through the blood of the Lamb;
    When my heart first believed,
    What a joy I received—
What a heaven in Jesus' name?

3 'Twas a heaven below
    My Redeemer to know,
And the angels could do nothing more
    Than to fall at his feet,
    And the story repeat,
And the Lover of sinners adore.

4 Jesus, all the day long,
    Was my joy and my song:
O that all his salvation might see;
    He hath loved me. I cried,
    He hath suffer'd and died,
To redeem even rebels like me.

* Or, "Home of the Soul," page 58.

INDEX.

Titles in SMALL CAPS; First Lines in Roman.

	Page		Page
ABIDE WITH ME	107	EVAN. C. M	121
A charge to keep I have	123	EVEN ME	102
Ah, tell me not of gold or treasure	79		
ALAS! AND DID MY SAVIOUR BLEED	13	FABER	108
ALETTA. 7s	105	Fade, fade each earthly joy	102
ALL FOR JESUS	63	FORREST. L. M	120
All glory to Jesus be given	32	FOR THOU HAST DIED FOR ME	30
All hail the power of Jesus' name	121	From every stormy wind that	109
ALL TO CHRIST I OWE	48	FULL SALVATION	101
ALMOST PERSUADED	81		
AND CAN IT BE?	93	GATE AJAR FOR ME	11
And can I yet delay	123	GERAR. S. M	122
Another fleeting day is gone	114	Give to the winds thy fears	122
Asleep in Jesus! blessed sleep!	113	GLORY TO THE LAMB!	17
A soft sweet voice from Eden	49	God is love, His mercy brightens	104
AT THE CROSS THERE'S ROOM	10	God loved the world of sinners	42
AVON. C. M	122	GUIDE. 7s. DOUBLE	60
AZMON. C. M	121	Guide me, O thou great Jehovah	99
BEAUTIFUL HOME OF THE BLEST	44	HAMBURG. L. M	90
BEAUTIFUL RIVER	68	HARP. C. M	112
Behold the Saviour of mankind	112	HEAVEN IS MY HOME	116
BELIEVER. C. M	90	Heavenly Father, bless me now	103
BELOVED. 11s & 8s	109	Heavenly Father, I would wear	105
BETHANY. 6s & 4s	125	HEBER. C. M	122
Beyond the smiling and the weeping	115	HE LEADETH ME	77
Blessed Jesus, blessed Jesus	43	Holy Spirit, faithful Guide	60
BLESS ME NOW	103	HOME OF THE SOUL	58
Blest be the tie that binds	116	HOW CAN I KEEP FROM SINGING?	22
BOYLSTON. S. M	123	How oft have I the Spirit grieved	99
Breaking through the clouds that	50	How sweet the name of Jesus	90
BRIGHT FOREVER	50		
BY THE GATE THEY'LL MEET US	33	I'M but a stranger here	116
By Thy birth, and by Thy tears	124	I AM COMING, LORD	86
		I am coming to the Cross	53
CAN my soul find rest from sorrow	45	I am far frae my hame, an' I'm	31
CARMARTHEN. H. M	124	I'M GOING HOME	62
CARRIE. 7s, 6s & 8s	96	I'M HAPPY, I'M HAPPY	87
CLEANSING FOUNTAIN	20	I'M KNEELING AT THE CROSS	18
CLEANSING WAVE	19	I am so glad that our Father in	91
Come, brethren, don't grow weary	54	I AM THE DOOR	27
COME, COME TO JESUS!	51	I AM THINE OWN	56
Come, humble sinner, in whose	122	I AM TRUSTING, LORD, IN THEE	53
COME NEARER, JESUS	104	I AM WAITING BY THE RIVER	82
Come, O thou Traveler unknown	64	I AM WAITING FOR THE SAVIOUR	98
Come ye that love the Lord	123	I COME TO THEE	47
CONSECRATION	72	IF I WERE A VOICE	118
CORONATION. C. M	121	IF TO JESUS FOR RELIEF	83
CROSS AND CROWN. C. M	112	I have entered the valley of blessing	12
		I hear the Saviour say	48
DEAR Jesus, I long to be perfectly	25	I hear thy welcome voice	86
Dear Lord, thy loving greatness	108	I KNOW THOU ART GONE	111
Depth of Mercy, can there be	124	I LOVE THEE	97
DUANE STREET. L. M	117	I LOVE TO TELL THE STORY	6

	Page		Page
I need Thee every hour	8	O for a thousand tongues to sing	121
In God I have found a retreat	34	Oh bliss of the purified! bliss of	24
In mercy, Lord, remember me	121	Oh, how He loves	37
In some way or other, the Lord	59	Oh, how sweet when we mingle	26
In the Christian's home in glory	95	Oh, now I see the crimson wave	19
In the Cross of Christ I glory	105	O how happy are they, Who their	125
In the fadeless Spring-time	33	Oh, sing of His Mighty Love	24
In the Rifted Rock I'm resting	14	Oh, sometimes the shadows are	66
I stand all bewildered with wonder	69	Old, old story	80
I thirst, thou wounded Lamb of God	120	Once more, my soul, the rising day	122
I will sing you a song of that	58	One more day's work for Jesus	55
		One there is above all others	37
Jesus, I my Cross have taken	76	Only just Across the River	106
Jesus is mighty to save	32	Only One Way to the Cross	35
Jesus is mine. 6s & 4s	102	Only Thee	71
Jesus, keep me near the Cross	78	Only Thee, my soul's Redeemer	71
Jesus, let thy pitying eye	96	Oron. 7s. 6 lines	124
Jesus, lover of my soul	125	Ortonville. C. M	122
Jesus loves even me	91	O sing to me of Heaven	67
Jesus, my all, to heaven is gone	117	O that my load of sin were gone	120
Jesus paid it all	40	O the sleep of just a moment	36
Jesus, Saviour, hear my call	107	O, think of a home over there	39
Jesus, thine all-victorious love	122	O Thou God of my Salvation	29
Just as I am, without one plea	90	O Thou, in whose presence my	109
		O Thou, to whose all searching sight	120
Kentucky. S. M	123	Our Loved Ones gone before	26
		O, when shall I sweep through the	15
Land ahead, its fruits are waving	9	O, who'll stand up for Jesus	57
Land of Beulah	52	O ye that are weary and laden	74
Let earth and heaven agree	124		
Let me go	110	Pass me not, O gentle Saviour	5
Light and Comfort of my Soul	38	Peacefully Rest	114
Like the Sound of many Waters	94	Penitence. 7s, 6s & 8s	96
Look, look to Jesus	87	Pilesgrove. L. M	120
Lord, I am thine. entirely thine	120	Pleyel's Hymn. 7s	124
Lord, I hear of showers of blessings	102	Prayer. 7s	124
Love of Jesus, all divine	92	Precious Jesus!	61
Loving Saviour, hear my cry	46	Precious Jesus, O, to love Thee	61
		Precious Name	8
Martyn. 7s. Double	125	Precious Saviour, thou hast saved	101
Mary Magdalen	89	Prince of my peace	69
Missionary Chant. L. M	120	Prince of Peace, control my will	124
More Love to Thee, O Christ	7		
Mourner, wheresoe'er thou art	10	Rathbun. 8s & 7s	105
Must Jesus bear the Cross alone?	112	Remember me. C. M	113
My Ain Countrie	31	Rest. L. M	113
My body, soul, and spirit	72	Rest for the Weary	95
My faith looks up to Thee	125	Resting at the Cross	28
My Goal is Christ	79	Rest in Thee	43
My God, my life, my love	123	Retreat. L. M	109
My heavenly home is bright and fair	62	Revive us again	57
My hope is built on nothing less	108	Rifted Rock	14
My latest sun is sinking fast	52	River of Song	36
My life flows on in endless song	22	Rock of Ages! cleft for me	124
My Saviour, my Almighty Friend	62	Rock that is Higher	66
Naught of merit or of price	40	Safe in the Arms of Jesus	4
Nearer, my God, to Thee	125	Safe within the Vail	9
Near the Cross	78	Saint Philip. S. M	116
New Haven. 6s & 4s	125	Save me at the Cross	46
Northfield. C. M	121	Secret Prayer	21
Nothing but Leaves	84	Sessions. L. M	120
		Shall we gather at the river	68
O for a closer walk with God	121	Shall we meet in Heaven	41
O for a heart to praise my God	121	Shirland. S. M	123

	Page		Page
Show pity, Lord, O Lord forgive.....	120	There is no friend like Jesus.........	70
SING TO ME OF HEAVEN..............	67	There is only one way to the cross...	35
Sinner, come, will you go?..........	56	THE RESURRECTION..................	53
SINNER INVITED.....................	56	THE RIFTED ROCK...................	14
Sinners, turn; why will ye die?.....	60	THE RIVER OF SONG.................	36
SOLID ROCK.........................	100	THE ROCK THAT IS HIGHER.........	66
SONG OF HOPE......................	49	THE SINNER INVITED................	56
STATE STREET. S. M................	123	THE SOLID ROCK....................	100
STEPHENS. C. M....................	121	THE SONG OF HOPE..................	49
SUPPLICATION. L. M. 6 lines........	124	THE SURRENDER....................	99
SURRENDER	99	THE SWEET BY-AND-BY..............	16
SWEET BY-AND-BY	16	THE TRUE FRIEND...................	70
SWEET REST.........................	74	THE VALLEY OF BLESSING...........	12
SWEET REST IN HEAVEN.............	54	The world is overcome by the........	17
SWEET HOUR OF PRAYER.............	75	THINE, LORD, FOREVER!.............	108
		Thou hidden source of calm..........	124
TAKE the name of Jesus with you...	8	Thou very present aid	123
TELL ME, JESUS.....................	85	TOPLADY. 7s. 6 lines	124
Tell me the old, old story...........	80	To the Cross of Christ, my..........	28
THATCHER. S. M...................	123	To the hall of the feast, came the.....	89
The angels that watched round.......	53	TRUE FRIEND	70
The blood, the blood is all my.......	18		
THE BLOOD, THE PRECIOUS BLOOD!..	73	UNDER HIS WINGS...................	34
THE BRIGHT FOREVER...............	50	UXBRIDGE. L. M...................	120
THE CLEANSING FOUNTAIN...........	20		
THE CLEANSING WAVE...............	19	VAIN, delusive world, adieu.........	96
THE CONVERT. 12s & 9s............	125	VALLEY OF BLESSING.............	12
THE CROSS..........................	65	VARINA. C. M. DOUBLE............	122
The Cross, the Cross! the blood.....	73		
THE DEAR ONES ALL AT HOME......	115	WE'VE A HOME OVER THERE.........	39
THE GATE AJAR FOR ME............	11	WELCOME TO GLORY.............	15
THE LAND OF BEULAH...............	52	We praise Thee, O God! for the......	57
THE LORD WILL PROVIDE...........	59	WE SHALL MEET....................	23
THE OLD, OLD STORY...............	80	What to me are earth's pleasures.....	26
THE PENITENT......................	45	When clouds hang darkly o'er ......·	30
THE PRECIOUS NAME................	8	When I survey the wondrous	65
THE PRINCE OF MY PEACE...........	69	WHITER THAN SNOW................	25
There is a fountain filled with.......	20	WHO'LL STAND UP FOR JESUS?......	57
There's a wideness in God's........	104	WINDHAM. L. M...................	120
There is a gate that stands ajar	11	WONDROUS LOVE....................	42
THERE'S A LAND FAR AWAY	88	WRESTLING JACOB	64
There is a land of pure delight.......	122		
There's a land that is fairer than.....	16	YE Christian heralds, go proclaim...	120
There is an hour of calm relief.......	21		

☞ *Most of the Hymns and Tunes in this Work are Copyright property, and can only be used by permission first obtained from the Authors or Publishers.*

WARREN, Music Stereotyper, 43 Centre St., N. Y.

www.ingramcontent.com/pod-product-compliance
Lightning Source LLC
Chambersburg PA
CBHW020113170426
43199CB00009B/515